THE ARSENAL STORY

AN
OFFICIAL

HISTORY OF
ARSENAL FOOTBALL CLUB

MICHAEL WADE

g

Lomond Books

A Grange Publication

© 1999

g Published by Grange Communications Ltd., Edinburgh, under licence from Arsenal Football Club.

Printed in the EU.

ISBN: 1-84204-006-5

CONTENTS

INTRODUCTION   5

THE GREATEST SIDE OF ALL?   7

LAYING THE FOUNDATIONS   17

GREAT NAMES   29

THE NEARLY YEARS   47

PICTURE GALLERY   83

INTRODUCTION

There's a feeling abroad that Arsenal, one of best-known clubs in world football, is about to enter its greatest phase. The side which has been moulded by Arsene Wenger achieved a 'double' in 1997-98, and a year later came within a whisker of another. As a thousand years of history closes, so a football side with over a hundred years experience seems equipped to scale new heights.

Success in Europe would arguably be the ultimate prize, but more than any of its predecessors this Arsenal side appears to have the ability to achieve it. This, in itself, is a remarkable testimony to the quality of this modern squad, for many of the Gunners line-ups from the past have touched greatness.

This book puts the achievements of today's Arsenal in perspective. First it analyses Wenger's tantalizing mix of English steel and mercurial European talent. Then, through a memorable history, it charts the almost irresistible rise of a great club.

True, there have been fallow periods - success rarely comes easily in football. But Highbury, and before it (to a lesser degree perhaps) Plumstead, more often than not has been a theatre in which many of football's finest talents have displayed their flamboyant skills.

Even in the earliest days, Arsenal had its share of stars - look at the early photographs of the side and some of its individual players to witness the pride that shines through the forefathers of the modern team.

But it was in the late 1920s and 1930s that the Gunners' reputation was forged, under the stewardship of inimitable manager Herbert Chapman and in the days of some of the greatest stars of the era, of any era - David Jack, Alex James, Cliff 'Boy' Bastin and Eddie Hapgood.

These heroes were succeeded by others and their dramatic domestic successes found a sonorous echo in the early 1970s' side of Bertie Mee, who claimed the Fairs Cup and were, at last, 'double' winners. Again, in manager George Graham's achievements, the side rose to standards rarely seen in the English game, to claim a sensational league title at Anfield.

Perhaps unsurprisingly, these successes on the field have been accompanied by a history off the field which has been by turn dramatic and beguiling. Through many generations, the club has nurtured some of the game's great characters - from chairman Henry Norris, who had the vision to move the club to its current North London home - through Chapman himself, and on to characters of the modern game, Graham and that inscrutable Frenchman, Wenger himself.

All of these personalities are writ large in the Arsenal story, as colourful a club history as any in the game.

The Greatest Side of All?

A Double won, in May 1998, and Peter Hill-Wood, Arsenal's chairman, summed up Arsène Wenger's contribution to the club. "He is just more intelligent than the rest of us. At least we have the sense to leave him to get on with the job and it would be fun to win the European Champions' League. We will make sure that Mr Wenger has the means to improve the team."

A year on and Hill-Wood's happy summation of the state of the club and of Wenger's contribution held good - how could it otherwise? True, in 1998/99, Arsenal had won nothing. But they had come within a whisker of two glorious triumphs in the major domestic competitions, taking Manchester United down to the very last game of the League season in their chase for the title and losing in the FA Cup semi final through a mixture of ill-luck - a missed penalty - and brilliance - Ryan Giggs' stunning solo goal. Two kicks from Wembley and a points tally which was superior to the total that won the side the league in the previous campaign: clearly, it's a thin line between success and failure.

Wenger's Arsenal is established, incontestably, as one of the three or four biggest clubs in the English game, who need fear no opponent at home or abroad. And where previous Arsenal sides - perhaps, just occasionally, with some justification - have been labelled 'boring' by the club's detractors, the Frenchman has produced a team whose dynamism and workrate has been matched by flamboyance and sublime skill to become one of the great sides of European football. How great has yet to proved on a wider stage but there is no doubt that this side bears comparison with all of the great Gunners teams that have preceded it … and that is greatness, indeed.

Early Doors

"There is something special about this team. They have a good camaraderie, because they have been playing together for a long time," said Arsene Wenger, after he had watched an impressive away win. In only his eighth game in charge of the club, Arsenal had beaten Newcastle at St James' Park and gone top of the Premiership. The Frenchman was already aware that the side he had inherited and that he was moulding, had the potential to be the best in Britain.

That season was to be the Gunners most impressive since George Graham left the club, as Arsenal finished third in the Premiership behind Manchester United and Newcastle. True, there was inconsistency, with defeats, for example, from Nottingham Forest and Wimbledon but some good away form kept the team mathematically in the race longer than might have been expected. More than that, with the maturing of Patrick Vieira, the signing for just £500,000 of Nicolas Anelka and the classic Arsenal back-line of Dixon, Adams, Keown or Bould and Winterburn, the side were set fair for far greater things in the future.

It was this matching of the skills of the existing side and the flair, often, it is true, imported from the continent, that the manager consistently strove to achieve. He had inherited a well-balanced outfit from Bruce Rioch's short 14-month reign as manager, one that had a settled and indefatigable defence and forwards, in Dennis Bergkamp and Ian Wright, probably unrivalled in the Premiership. In those early days of his management, the Frenchman astutely recognised that he had to reassure the players who were already at Highbury and mix them with the talents he felt could be added to the squad to build a world-class club side.

"Every manager has his own way of working and it is always difficult for players to accept a new code of behaviour," he said of those early days. "I wouldn't say I caused a revolution, it is more of a mixture. The players had to adapt and I had to adapt, to create a new balance."

Ian Wright: beat 'Boy' Bastin's scoring record for Arsenal.

Building Success

Wenger's arrival was timely. His knowledge of the world game - from his coaching days in Monaco to his sojourn in Japan and every experience of football in between - had exposed him to some of the best talents in the game. Just at the moment when the standard of English domestic football had been driven to almost unexpected heights, here was a manager with the vision to build on a grander scale than had been possible before.

His summer's work before the 1997/98 season, in part at least, was taken up with capturing those talents he felt were most suited to the Arsenal cause. Marc Overmars, the flying Dutch winger who had destroyed England's World Cup qualifying campaign in 1993, was one such target. Out of the Ajax team through injury for much of the previous season, he was keen to prove his fitness at the top level. He duly came to Highbury.

His signing was followed by a raft of others - defender Gilles Grimandi and midfielder Emmanuel Petit, both from Wenger's former club, Monaco; two young strikers followed, Christopher Wreh and Luis Boa Morte, both of whom were to become vital elements of the Arsenal squad.

Emmanuel Petit, of course, was to achieve so much more and become a vital cog in the side. Wenger has been unstinting in his praise. "I bought him firstly because he is a team-minded player. His first concern is always, 'How can I help the team?' That is why he is not the most spectacular player but he is always a very valuable one. Of course, I knew him from my time at Monaco, where he was a defender. I knew he was a generous character with a strong physical ability to run and run.

"From the physical point of view, I knew he could play in midfield and when he played as a defender, facing the play, he was always dangerous with his long passes. Also because of the physical intensity of English football, I wanted someone to help Vieira to fight. I thought Patrick was outstanding last season (1996-97) but if we lost him suspended or injured, it was always a question of who would play. I knew Petit and Vieira would suit each other because one is left-footed and the other right and one passes the ball short, the other long. It has worked very well."

With so many coming in, some critics suggested that Wenger was in danger of abandoning the English heart of the team, as near-neighbours, Chelsea, had done. For the Frenchman, however, the importance of that element of the club could not have been stronger. By mid season, his only problem, he said, with a large part of his English contingent, was simply their age.

"That is my biggest headache. It is not just a question of replacing the quality of their play but also the quality of their English spirit," he said. "They are all English and I want to keep an English base to the team. I have bought foreign players but it is important to keep the good things that come from an English approach. We must keep that old Arsenal spirit.

"Tony Adams is the natural leader of the team, through his personality and his performance and he has the respect of everybody.

"All these defenders are an exceptional bunch, spirit-wise. We can help them to prolong their careers, through diet and exercise but the main thing that keeps them going is their own motivation."

Dennis Bergkamp - bought by Bruce Rioch – has continued to flourish under Arsene Wenger's management.

Double Delight

But it was another old Highbury favourite who got Wenger's first, extraordinary full season in 1997-98 off to the greatest of beginnings. Ian Wright earned the Gunners a draw at Leeds, and then scored twice in the next fixture at home to Coventry, to move within a goal of Cliff 'Boy' Bastin's goal-scoring record for the club. It took another month for Wright to achieve that target and in between times, Dennis Bergkamp had already caught fire, with brilliant displays at Southampton and Leicester.

However, at this early stage of the campaign, Arsenal faltered. They departed from the UEFA Cup in their first tie at the hands of PAOK Salonika and had their first league defeat at Derby County. A 3-2 home victory over Manchester United improved morale but it was swiftly followed by defeat at Highbury by an impressive Blackburn Rovers. At New Year, with the Gunners trailing United by 12 points, critics in the press suggested that Wenger was failing to achieve the requisite blend and that players had formed national cliques within the camp. He was dismissive:

"If I was to bring two or three Irish players here, they would stick together, as do Bould and Adams, who have been partners for years but that doesn't mean they don't like the others. It's just natural," he said. "Vieira speaks more with Petit than with Adams because communication is easier but Vieira puts his foot in for Adams on the field. That's what is important.

"The word clique has a negative connotation. It is not like that. In the past, I have had teams where the players did not get on with each other and you could feel the tension. I don't feel it here at all. They get angry at each other because they are frustrated at not winning when they should. You cannot expect players to be happy when they lose."

He was right: the mood began to lift at the club, as Arsenal began to win. They staggered past Port Vale in the third round of the FA Cup, needing a replay and penalties to settle the issue but their League form and Manchester United's unaccustomed inconsistency saw them gaining on their main rivals for the title. A turning point came at Old Trafford, as Arsenal secured their first 'double' of the season - over the Champions - and that success achieved after Nicolas Anelka set up Marc Overmars, was the second in a glorious run of ten straight wins.

As the run came to a crescendo, the Gunners defeated Newcastle 3-1 to go top and then swept imperiously past Blackburn and Wimbledon, scoring five against the former and four against the latter. After a narrow victory over Derby, only Everton barred their way to the title - and that with three games still to come. The critical game was almost embarrassingly easy - the Gunners sent on their way in only six minutes by an own-goal from Stefan Bilic, with Marc Overmars cashing in either side of half time. It seemed only fitting that one of Arsenal's finest servants, Tony Adams, should score the goal that put the game and the Championship beyond doubt.

After their travails against Port Vale, the FA Cup seemed to get no easier. West Ham took the Gunners to penalties in the quarter finals, after Crystal Palace had required a replay. But in the semi final against First Division Wolves, Arsenal superiority was never seriously questioned in a 1-0 win.

The final, too, was never a contest; neutrals bemoaned its one-sidedness. After Anelka had spurned a couple of opportunities, Marc Overmars fired the Gunners into the lead. Newcastle, who surrendered the middle of the field to Vieira and Petit with an astonishing lack of fight, created nothing for their centre forward Alan Shearer and their efforts on goal were almost embarrassingly limited. When Anelka seized on a Parlour pass, his galloping run and drive past Newcastle goalkeeper Shay Given put the game beyond doubt with 22 minutes still remaining. There was no way back for the Geordies. Arsenal had collected a 'double' for the first time since Bertie Mee's great side.

Wenger had no doubt about the significance of that Wembley victory and the achievement it secured for him - the first overseas manager to lead an English 'double'-winning side. He described it as "the greatest moment of my sporting life."

True, he had been worried about a slipshod build-up to the FA Cup Final but after the event he was glowing. "We had lost concentration after winning the title but we have been remarkable this season. We kept getting better and so has the mixture between the foreign and English players."

Nearly men

After achieving a fabulous 'double' in May 1998, the outcome in 1998-99 was doubly disappointing for the Gunners, as the side came within a hair's breadth of repeating that fantastic feat.

In the Premiership, often playing truly thrilling football, the club secured 78 points, more than the tally that had been enough to win the trophy the previous season. It was a terrific performance, enough to push the eventual winners, Manchester United, down to the wire - and over the second half of the campaign, the Gunners were arguably the better side. In the FA Cup, Arsenal fought through to the semi finals before missing a penalty and then going out to a magnificent solo goal by United's Ryan Giggs in a replay at Villa Park.

But in the final analysis, it was probably the side's form in the first four months of the season that cost them dear. Despite two 3-0 triumphs over their Manchester rivals - one of them in the season's curtain-raiser, the Charity Shield - Arsenal contrived to lose sloppy games against Wimbledon and Sheffield Wednesday and drop points to another struggling side, Charlton.

It was a period, too, in which the club's Champions League challenge came unstuck. After unluckily drawing in Lens and defeating Panathinaikos at Wembley, injuries - and Dennis Bergkamp's fear of flying - cost the side dearly, as Arsenal drew at home with Dynamo Kiev, before losing the second fixture with both the Russian side and Lens. Those results - and a 0-5 pounding at Chelsea in the League Cup – cast a long shadow at Highbury.

It says everything about the side that Arsene Wenger has built that they were able to put these disappointments behind them. In the run-up to the New Year, the Gunners defeated Leeds, Charlton and West Ham, the beginning of a run that saw the club go unbeaten in 19 games, until an unlucky defeat at Elland Road in the penultimate game of the season.

In that time, there were many memorable games. There were magnificent, sweeping performances such as the 5-0 demolition of Leicester City. There was controversy in the goal by Nwankwo Kanu, which appeared to have knocked Sheffield United out of the FA Cup, before Arsenal sportingly agreed to replay the game. There was sweet victory over local rivals, Spurs, 3-1 at White Hart Lane and one of the goals of the season - of *any* season - by Kanu.

And when Arsenal powered away at the top of the Premiership with five goals against Wimbledon and six at Middlesbrough in successive games, it seemed that the club could retain the title. Only a hard-fought defeat at Leeds cost Arsenal the crown - and there, a dramatic goal-line clearance by Jonathon Woodgate decisively denied the Gunners.

There was much to admire in some thrilling football; much to build on, in the world-class performances of Tony Adams, Emmanuel Petit and Bergkamp; much to hope for, as another Champions' League challenge beckons. The basis of the side is there already in the powerhouse defence, though Wenger is as alert as anyone to the ageing of that element of the side. He is on record as admiring the youth system at Old Trafford but has argued for patience among the fans, who may wish to see similar home-grown talent come through:

"You have got to realise that Manchester United have put ten years' work into getting where they are, dominating English football - ten years! We will try to develop the same way but remember, for five of those ten years they didn't win anything. Would any manager be given so long today? I doubt it. Lose three games and they want to start a revolution."

There will be no revolution. Already Ray Parlour and Matthew Upson have burst on to the Arsenal stage; more English stars will follow. Wenger will continue his magic mix and for now, the team still combines that solidity, almost serenity at the back, with the dynamism of Vieira and Petit in the midfield and the brilliance of Bergkamp, Overmars and Kanu in attack.

Not a bad outlook for the side who came second in 1999. Let the good times roll.

Laying the Foundations

A Club is Born

There is a curious similarity between the Arsenal of today and the Royal Arsenal side that preceded it over 100 years ago. Just as the modern team features many players who are making their livings far from the places where they were brought up, so too did that original side. Royal Arsenal was formed in 1886, not by Frenchmen or Italians or Africans, but by men from the Midlands, the North of England and Scotland, all of whom had arrived in London to work.

The very first Arsenal side was, in effect, a works side, formed by people who earned their livings in a vast munitions factory. Originally the team bore the name of the area of the Arsenal where the men worked - Dial Square FC - but within a couple months and just one game, that was changed. The historic day was Christmas Day 1886, when footballers led by the captain and organiser, David Danskin, met in a pub called the Royal Oak, in Woolwich. They agreed to incorporate part of the pub's name into that of the team and the Royal Arsenal football club was born.

The first Arsenal football team owed more than its name to this place of work - the vast munitions factory helped to supply a steady flow of players, too. In the latter part of the 19th century, the factory was probably as busy as it ever had been, producing weaponry to bolster the forces of the British Empire and caught up in the escalating arms race that preceded the First World War. It was, throughout the period, a major employer and a magnet for workers from industrial Britain, who often brought their passion for football with them. Two of first stars of the side, Fred Beardsley and Morris Bates, had played for Nottingham Forest - and had probably worked in the Nottingham Ordnance factory, too. Apart from anything else, their connections helped to secure the club a set of red shirts, which for nearly 50 years were the side's trademark. Forest also kindly sent the new London club a ball to play with.

The new side played their first game on 8 January 1897, against Erith on Plumstead Common, a game they won easily, 6-1. Eight more matches followed, five wins, two defeats and a draw - the Second Rifle Brigade put up the toughest opposition, drawing one game with Royal Arsenal and winning another.

There were no leagues to play in through those early seasons and instead, the Royal Arsenal side took part in friendly matches or in any one of a handful of cups that were organised in

London and the South East of England. In these, the club became increasingly successful, in 1889/90 winning the London Charity Cup, the Kent Senior Cup and the Kent Junior Cup. That year they also appeared for the first time in the FA Cup, defeated 5-1 by Swifts in the last of the qualifying rounds.

In the following season, came the club's first major success - a 6-0 victory over St Bartholemew's Hospital in the final of the London Senior Cup. The reporter for the Kentish Examiner captured some of the atmosphere after a famous victory: "Excitement is a mild description for the scenes in Woolwich and Plumstead on the return of the football champions on Saturday night," he wrote. "A host of admirers met them at the Dockyard Station and drove them in open carriages, shouting and singing. There were celebrations everywhere, all evening and we fear a good deal of drinking was mixed with the rejoicing and exultation."

That year, the club's members took a momentous decision - to turn professional. It was a move greeted with horror by the London FA, who expelled them and Arsenal also found themselves barred from the southern cup competitions.

Instead, the side were forced to play teams from the Midlands and the North and with hindsight, it may be that this exposure to more experienced and professional sides helped the Londoners develop their game. Certainly, results in 1891 and 1892, when they lost heavily to Sheffield Wednesday, Preston North End and Wolverhampton Wanderers, must have been chastening. The following year, a home victory over Sheffield United suggested better days ahead - and by September 1893, Arsenal found themselves fully paid-up members of the Football League.

1893: it was a historic year. Based at the Manor Ground, which was to be their home for the next 20 years, the club had now been incorporated as The Woolwich Arsenal Football and Athletic Club. And now battle commenced in the Second Division, with a 2-2 draw at home to Newcastle United. Arsenal were the only league club to be found south of Birmingham.

Royal Arsenal in summer, 1890, with the rewards of a fabulous Treble, the London Charity Cup, the Kent Senior Cup and the Kent Junior Cup. The team's founder, David Danksin from Kirkcaldy, is second left on the front row, sitting on the ground.

Caesar Augustus Llewelyn Jenkyns, who joined Arsenal in 1895, was the first serving member of an Arsenal side to play international football, when he was selected at centre half for Wales.

Woolwich Arsenal

The first seasons in the Second Division met with only limited success for Woolwich Arsenal, with the side achieving the kind of mid-table respectability that hardly seems to satisfy fans these days. The club experimented with the notion of a professional manager, appointing one in each of the seasons from 1897-1899. The first two, TB Mitchell and George Elcoat, lasted a season each but the third, Harry Bradshaw, was to stay for five years and guide the club to its first league success, runners-up in 1903/04 and promotion to the First Division.

Again limited success followed, with the Gunners fighting their way through to FA Cup semi finals in 1906 and 1907, only to be defeated by Newcastle United and Sheffield Wednesday respectively. However, by the end of the first decade of the century, the club faced a financial crisis off the field and the threat of relegation on it.

That the Reds (so they had been nicknamed from the earliest days) survived was almost entirely thanks to the efforts of Henry Norris, a director who was that rare thing, a real football man and one who was to become Arsenal chairman. Originally the chairman of Fulham, Norris was determined to forge a London side capable of taking on the old-established sides of the Football League. Originally, he intended to merge the two clubs, or at least have the sides ground-share at Craven Cottage, Fulham's ground. However, when he took his seat on the Arsenal board, Norris appears to have made up his mind to use Woolwich Arsenal - still a First Division club – as the vehicle to drive his dream.

Alas, Norris faced his first major setback in 1912/13, when the side was relegated, after a dreadful season in which they won only one home game all season. It was a disaster that prompted the chairman to radical action.

Unhappy with the level of support the side were receiving in Plumstead - the most obvious reason for the club's parlous financial state - Norris hit upon the idea of moving the club's home, to make it more central and easier to reach for larger numbers of supporters. Norris found the site he wanted at Highbury: it was near an Underground station and at the heart of a densely populated area.

At first, the club paid £20,000 to lease the ground for 21 years from St John's College of Divinity and the deed of transfer was signed by the Archbishop of Canterbury. Norris almost immediately spent another £125,000 building a grandstand and terraces at the site. It was, according to Bob Wall, one of the club's most loyal servants, "in many ways, the most astute single decision ever taken by the club".

The club made an encouraging start in their new surroundings. Woolwich was officially dropped from the club's name and in their first game at Highbury, on 6 September 1913, Arsenal beat Leicester Fosse 2-1. It began a good season for the side and Norris must have hoped that he would be rewarded by promotion to the more lucrative First Division. He was not: the Reds finished third, bettered only on goal difference by second-placed club, Bradford Park Avenue.

Woolwich Arsenal FC, season 1897-98.

Plain Old Arsenal

It seemed, after the four terrible years of the First World War, that Arsenal would have to begin again their fight to return to the First Division. The player pool, which might once have secured promotion in 1915/16, had aged and been depleted. Left to themselves, the players might have found the task of stepping up a flight too tough to tackle successfully.

In the event, the team and its fans owed a controversial promotion back to Division One to chairman Norris. By now a Tory MP and a knight, Sir Henry appears to have had the charm and persuasive powers to ensure that League officials, who were poised to expand the First Division from 20 to 22 clubs, should promote Arsenal from the Second Division. That he could do so was all the more remarkable, since Arsenal had finished fifth in Division Two in the final pre-war season, while Spurs, the side demoted to Division Two to accommodate the Highbury club, had finished twentieth in Division One.

The final outcome saw Derby County and Preston North End, first and second in Division Two, promoted as expected, Chelsea, nineteenth in Division One in the 1914/15 season, re-elected and Spurs replaced by Arsenal, after Arsenal received 18 votes to Spurs' 8 in the Football League meeting. The reason cited for Arsenal's promotion was the club's service to the league and its longevity - a more spurious claim could hardly have been imagined, since Wolves, who finished fourth, were four years older than Arsenal. Norris's diplomatic skills, we must imagine, were great, indeed, to pull off such a coup. So, promoted they were - and the fact of Arsenal's good fortune, combined with the relegation of local rivals, Spurs, was the cause of great bitterness between the two clubs.

A new era was being ushered in for the club. Norris appointed Leslie Knighton as manager, a young man who arrived with a big reputation for his work at Huddersfield Town and Manchester City. His task was to build a team without spending a fortune on transfer fees - Norris was all too well aware of the club's financial position and unwilling to gamble in the face of rapidly rising transfer fees. He capped Knighton's spending, insisting that no more than £1,000 was spent on any single player.

Knighton proved adept at fulfilling part of the job. Such were his persuasive powers, that top-quality stars such as Welsh international left half, Bob John and all-rounder, Alf Baker, chose Arsenal above a handful of interested clubs when they came on to the transfer market.

But the strictures imposed by a tight cash regime proved too great for Knighton. In six years, the highest league position achieved by the club was ninth, while in no season did 'goals for' exceed 'goals against'. In November 1925, with the club out of the FA Cup and in twentieth position in the league, Norris advertised in *The Athletic News* for a new manager.

Arsenal Honours 1886-1925

1889/90	London Charity Cup; Kent Senior Cup; Kent Junior Cup
1890/91	London Senior Cup
1896/97	Kent Senior Cup; Kent County League
1901/02	London Football League; West Kent League
1902/03	West Kent League
1903/04	London Football League
1905/06	South Eastern League
1906/07	South Eastern League; London Football League
1907/08	South Eastern League
1921/22	London FA Challenge Cup
1922/23	London Combination
1923/24	London FA Challenge Cup

Arsenal Managers, 1897-1925:

Thomas B Mitchell, 1897-98

George Elcoat, 1898-99

Harry Bradshaw, 1899-1904

George Morrell, 1908-1915

Leslie Knighton, 1919-1925

The Most Famous in the World

"He knew when to blow you up and when to blow you down, when to be the Big Boss and when to be the Family Friend. He was a genius and that's the fact of it."

Few would disagree with Alex Jackson's assessment of Herbert Chapman, the manager who made Arsenal the most famous club football team in the world.

His arrival at Highbury came after Chapman had weathered a brilliant but controversial career in management, first at Northampton and then at Leeds City, where a corruption scandal blighted his work. He was to re-emerge at Huddersfield Town (for whom he signed the brilliant Jackson, who spoke so warmly of him), a club he guided to two First Division Championships and the FA Cup.

In 1925, at the age of 47, persuaded by Sir Henry Norris and by an annual salary of £2,000, Chapman arrived in North London to begin the complete transformation of the club. In just nine years he had built the most successful side that had ever been seen in English football.

An early photo of Herbert Chapman's Arsenal. Charles Buchan is pictured with the ball and Chapman sits on the right.

Team Building

As soon as he was appointed, Chapman set about convincing Sir Henry Norris that he should reverse his policy on transfer fees and he quickly identified the players whom he believed would form the foundation of a successful side. The veto of £1,000 imposed on his predecessor, Knighton, was soon forgotten, as Chapman bid £2,000 for Sunderland's 34-year-old forward, Charlie Buchan. The deal included an extra £100 for each goal Buchan scored over the first 12 months of his Arsenal career. Next, he signed the Hibernian goalkeeper, Bill Harper, for the princely sum of £5,000. The spending paid dividends, too: in Chapman's first season in charge, Arsenal finished second in Division One, behind Champions, Newcastle.

But the spree was only just beginning. Right winger, Joe Hulme - said to be the fastest man in football - arrived from Blackburn Rovers for £3,500. Charlie Jones, signed from Nottingham Forest, was to run up the left flank, while a former miner, Jack Lambert, was signed from Doncaster Rovers for £2,000, to add menace to the forward line. A great side was taking shape.

The Great Tactician

As a coach, Chapman was a genuine innovator and effectively helped create the game we know today, pioneering completely new tactics. The foundation of the Arsenal side became its 'stopper', a player whose sole job was to reinforce the side's defence. The role was developed after a change in the offside law in 1925, which had led to increased pressure on defences.

In fact, the idea of the 'stopper' was not Chapman's alone but the brainchild of Buchan, his respected senior player. Buchan had argued for some time that the Gunners' centre half, Jack Butler, should be used solely as a defender. After a crushing 7-0 defeat away to Newcastle, Chapman agreed to try out the plan, partly in response to Buchan's threat to leave the club if he did not.

Arsenal first used a 'stopper' against West Ham in an away match in October 1925 and won the game 4-0. Buchan must have been doubly delighted - he scored two of the goals, with another former coal miner, James Brain, claiming the other pair.

Chapman was quick to realise the potential of such tactics and his side soon established themselves as one to watch. The manager realised that building foundations meant solidity at the back: "It is laid down by law that the team who scores the most goals wins," he once said. "To accomplish, this you must make sure that the defence is sound."

Further innovation followed, as the manager developed the system which became known as the 'WM' formation, the system that drove Arsenal to success: fullbacks moved wide to cover opposition wingers; a second inside forward was moved back between the midfield line and the forwards; fast and skilful wingers were played, to cut in and attack from both left and right flanks; and in attack, three very fast forwards were left up front to torment opposition defences.

It relied heavily on quality players and Chapman had the nouse, and the financial support of the club to ensure he acquired or developed the talents he needed.

Wingers were vitally important, as was a playmaker in midfield. Joe Hulme, previously with York and Blackburn and reputedly the fastest man in British football, was signed by Chapman in 1926 to patrol one of the flanks. Three years later, he was to sign 17-year-old winger, Cliff Bastin, a young man who was destined to win every major honour in the English game by the time he was 19. And in the middle of the park, he had the incomparable Alex James.

Chapman's team was designed on a pivotal principle, as he himself explained: "First, as to attack, we have ceased to use our wing forwards in the old style, in which they hugged the touchline. Not only is it the aim of Hulme and Bastin to come inside when the Arsenal attack but also the aim of the wing halves. This gives us seven men going up on goal. Now, as to defence, the team swings the other way but the same principles apply, so we have eight defenders when the goal is challenged. The defence pivots towards the position of attack, the opposite back coming in to support the centre. It is, of course, essential that the two insides should come back and it is on this account that you get what is called the 'W' formation. The two wing halves are, therefore, the key men, either in defence or attack and no defence can be sound unless it has the support of the inside forwards."

Chapman had a shrewd notion of the counter-attack, too: "A team can attack for too long, though I do not suggest that the Arsenal go on the defensive, even for tactical purposes. I think it may be said that some of their best scoring chances have come when they have been driven back and then have broken away to strike suddenly and swiftly."

Great Names
Alex James

Chapman's search for a linking midfield player came to an end when Preston North End put former Raith Rovers player, Alex James, on the transfer list in 1929, for £9,000. James was seen at the time as a goalscorer but Chapman was convinced he had the right man for the middle of the park.

George Allison, who succeeded Chapman as manager, was to say of James: "No-one like him ever kicked a ball. He had a most uncanny and wonderful control but because this was allied to a split-second thinking apparatus, he simply left the opposition looking on his departing figure with amazement."

The Scot became the key to the team. Before his arrival, Arsenal had won nothing; by the time he left, they had won virtually everything. The system which Chapman deployed depended on him; but the style with which James executed his role was all his own.

Alex James brings the FA Cup back to Islington in 1930.

Cliff Bastin

The last of Chapman's great discoveries, the 17-year-old 'Boy' Bastin was spotted by the manager playing for Exeter City at Watford. Impressed, he set out almost at once to conclude a deal of £2,000 for the left winger.

Arriving at Highbury just two weeks after James, Bastin, too, emerged as man in a class of his own. Supreme in teasing and worrying defences, he possessed a sledgehammer shot and a famously calm demeanour. Tom Whittaker said of Bastin: "Coupled with his sincerity and his loyalty to all his bosses, he had a trait few of us are blessed with - that is, he had an ice-cold temperament."

With Hulme on the other flank, the triangle of Bastin/James/Hulme became Arsenal's unstoppable combination, as Sir Matt Busby, who played against the Gunners for Manchester City, once recalled. "James was the great creator from the middle," said Busby. "From an Arsenal rearguard action, the ball would, seemingly inevitably, reach Alex. He would feint and leave two or three opponents sprawling or plodding in his wake before he released the ball, unerringly, to either the flying Joe Hulme, who would not even have to pause in flight, or the absolutely devastating Cliff 'Boy' Bastin, who would take a couple of strides and whip the ball into the net."

Cliff 'Boy' Bastin.

Eddie Hapgood

In 1927, Chapman added finesse to the defence when he bought Eddie Hapgood, a former milkman, from Kettering Town. At only 19, Hapgood had been turned down by his home town club, Bristol Rovers, for being too small and slight to make it in the physical world of football. That was a profound misjudgement - Hapgood went on to captain Arsenal and played 30 times for England.

Hapgood was a physical fitness fanatic, a vegetarian a non-smoker (a rarity among footballers, then) and a non-drinker (a rarity among footballers now), who was, indeed, small enough to be knocked out from time to time by the heavy leather ball that was used in the 1920s and 1930s. It is said that Chapman persuaded him to eat steak to help Hapgood build up his strength.

But the great defender's admiration for Chapman was unstinting. "Herbert Chapman was a father figure," said Hapgood in an interview in 1966. "He was so clever at getting the players to talk about how they felt on the field and saying how they should have done this and done that. He just took himself away from the meeting, as it were, and let the boys get on with their tactical talks and then, suddenly, he would come in, make himself felt and say: 'Boys, I think that's it now - this is what we'll do – we'll go out on to the field and practise it.'"

David Jack

Charlie Buchan, Chapman's first signing, was a great attacking player - but in football terms, at 34, a veteran. When, in 1928, he left the club to take up a career in journalism, the free-scoring Buchan left a huge hole. David Jack, an accomplished inside forward with Bolton Wanderers, was the manager's chosen replacement.

Bolton were adamant that Jack was not for sale, setting a price of £13,000 - twice the existing transfer record in Britain. It was important to get the price down and Bob Wall, Chapman's secretary, recalled how the manager went about coaxing the Bolton management team, who came to London to discuss terms.

"We arrived at the hotel half an hour before our appointment. Chapman immediately went into the lounge bar. He called the waiter, placed two pound notes in his hand and said: 'George. This is Mr Wall, my assistant. He will drink whisky and dry ginger. I will drink gin and tonic. We shall be joined by guests. They will drink whatever they like. But I want you to be careful of one thing. See that our guests are given double of everything but Mr Wall's whisky and dry ginger will contain no whisky and my gin and tonic will contain no gin.'

"When the Bolton pair arrived, Chapman ordered the drinks. We quickly downed ours and he called for the same again. The drinks continued to flow and our guests were soon in a gay mood.

"Finally, when Chapman decided the time was opportune for talking business, they readily agreed to letting him sign Jack - and for £10,890, which we considered a bargain.

"Never did ginger ale and tonic water leave two persons so elated. When we were safely in our taxi on the return journey to Highbury, Chapman exclaimed: 'Well, that's your first lesson in football. You now know how to conduct a transfer.'"

Jack, who was to play 181 league games for Arsenal, scoring 113 goals and who became the first Arsenal player to captain England, was to justify his fee, prompting Chapman to later remark, "One of the best bargains I ever made was the most costly one."

The First Success

Chapman's tactical discussions with Buchan in October 1925 quickly paid dividends. From a side struggling against relegation, the Gunners made rapid strides and finished as high as they ever had in the First Division, second to Champions, Newcastle United. The club came within 90 minutes of success in 1927, when in their first FA Cup Final they lost 1-0 to Cardiff, in the year that the FA Cup left England for the only time (thus far) in its history.

But as the squad grew stronger and the tactics were honed, it seemed it could only be a matter of time before Chapman's side claimed a prize and in 1930, it came. For the manager, there was a double satisfaction in an FA Cup final appearance. Not only had he guided Arsenal there but their opponents, Huddersfield, still bore the master's stamp both in their personnel and in their tactical style.

The Gunners' victory was set up in the 16th minute by a typically quick bit of thinking by Alex James. Fouled by Goodall, the Scot placed the ball on the ground and played it swiftly to Bastin without even straightening himself up. The winger beat a man and then passed inside to James, who slipped the ball home.

Ronald Allen was a journalist who watched the game. He wrote: "Some discussion as to whether he took the free kick before he had been signalled to do so by the referee was disposed of by Mr Tom Crew, the official in charge, who said later on that James had made a raised-eyebrows appeal for permission to take the kick and Mr Crew waved him on. Quick thinking. James was good at that.

"If there was one quality James possessed, it was his individuality. There has never been another footballer like him. There never will be. He was short, stocky, puckish looking, impudent in the daring with which he ambled and shuffled and held on to the ball until he had the other side baffled and exasperated and wondering what he was going to do with it. He was the supreme football jester. Only a genius can get away with that.

"Having scored one goal, James flung ahead the long, raking perfectly judged pass in the wide open space he had created to make it inevitable that Yorkshireman, Jack Lambert, should score the second goal to a win a final everybody there will always remember."

Arsenal, who had many talented forwards during the thirties, probably had their greatest attacking formation in this match. It comprised Joe Hulme who could make crowds "sway like ripe corn in a half gale", so wrote one admiring journalist, David Jack, 'Honest' Jack Lambert, James and Bastin, whose instinctive relationship with the Scot was a cornerstone of the side's success.

It might be remarked that, on the day, Huddersfield had an awesome enough side of their own. WH Smith was on the left wing, a veteran of 17 seasons with the club but a man who was said to play with the spirit and pace of someone half his age. Smith helped to inspire a storming second-half comeback, aided and abetted by the man on the opposite wing, Alex Jackson. The star of the 1928 'Wembley wizards', the Scottish side that defeated England 5-1, Jackson had scored nine of the 11 goals that had brought Huddersfield to Wembley. This time, however, Wembley proved a fruitless visit for the Scot.

Looking back on the 1930s, Eddie Hapgood picked this as the greatest single Arsenal performance: "[We were] getting that team spirit that is necessary for any team to be successful," he recalled. "We were beginning to be called great."

Filling the Trophy Cabinet

That first Wembley success was rapidly followed by the arrival of other silverware. Within 12 months, Arsenal had become the first southern side to win the First Division Championship and did so with a record 66 points.

The season represented a great achievement for the Gunners. An amazing away record - won 14, drawn 5, lost 2, identical to their performance at home - set new First Division records for matches won and points scored away from home. Their tally of 60 away goals was a new league record - no team from any of the four divisions had ever scored more than 50 before. Amazingly, their huge total tally of 127 was bettered by runners-up, Aston Villa, who scored 128 and even put five past Chapman's men in mid-March. The Gunners only failed to score in one game - against Huddersfield at Highbury on 7 March - coincidentally, the only game in which they kept a clean sheet.

The next season began with optimistic talk of a 'double'. In the end, Arsenal won nothing. The club's league challenge was undermined by a disastrous series of results in March and early April, which allowed eventual winners, Everton, to open up a seven-point gap, thanks largely to their free-scoring centre forward, Dixie Deans, who claimed 44 goals that season.

There seemed to be, however, the consolation of an FA Cup to look forward to. This time, however, fortune did not favour 'Lucky' Arsenal in the final. Their hopes were dashed after they were defeated by Newcastle 2-1 and that after Bob John had given the Gunners an early lead. It was not a great Cup Final by any means but went down in history as one of the most controversial, because of Newcastle's bitterly-contested equaliser. When Jimmy Richardson chased the ball to the by-line, it seemed to have gone out of play before he crossed for Jack Allen to shoot and score from close range. The Arsenal defence certainly thought so, as they made no attempt to stop the Newcastle forward. The referee, Mr WP Harper, was unrepentant: "It was a goal ... as God is my judge, the ball was in play. I was eight yards away." The newsreel showed otherwise - the ball was out and Mr Harper 20 yards away.

Arsenal, without the injured James, struggled on through the rest of the game, before Allen struck the decisive goal in the 71st minute.

After that disappointment, Chapman decided against the wholesale restructuring of the side. Veteran, Tom Parker, however, was replaced at fullback by George Male (who had made his FA Cup debut in the final against Newcastle) and his partnership with Hapgood proved one of the most successful and enduring in the game.

A Double denied by Walsall?

Arsenal began the next season as if determined to erase the unhappy memories of Wembley. On Christmas Eve, they thumped nine goals past Sheffield United to go top of the league, on the way to scoring 118 goals over the season.

Just halfway through the campaign, many believed that the league was assured. All that remained was the cup and in the third round, only Second Division Walsall stood in the way. Coming into the game, the Arsenal squad were suffering from flu and three of the team's stalwarts - Hapgood, John and Lambert - fell victim to it. Joe Hulme's form was a concern, too and the manager elected to leave him out of the side. In for Lambert and Hulme, as Cliff Bastin remembered, Mr Chapman chose, respectively, Charlie Walsh and Billy Warnes. In doing so, he made two of his rare mistakes.

"Warnes," wrote Bastin, "was entirely the wrong kind of player for such a match as we were going to play. Essentially an artistic footballer, robust methods were liable to shake him off his game."

As for Walsh, Bastin was scathing: "He had long been trying to bring Chapman around to his own way of thinking - that he was the best centre forward on Arsenal's books - so far, without much success. In this match, however, Chapman gave him his chance. He missed it, all too emphatically."

The gruelling game plan that Walsall adopted immediately took its toll on the Gunners. "Almost as soon as play had started, it became clear to me that all our fears about the tactics our opponents might employ were fully justified," wrote Bastin. "Walsall could not have complained had five of their men, at least, been sent off the field in the first quarter of an hour. Arsenal were awarded ten free kicks in as many minutes after the first whistle. Do not misinterpret me. I don't want to level an indictment at the Walsall players. They played, a little too vigorously perhaps but their game, which was right in the circumstances.

"Yet for all Walsall's crude tactics and for all the difficulties imposed by the tiny pitch and the proximity of the spectators who sat round it, I still say we should have won. We had enough chances to bang in half a dozen goals. Not one was accepted.

"Charlie Walsh was the chief offender. His nervousness was pitiable to behold. On one occasion during the first half, I crossed the ball right on to his head, with not one Walsall defender standing within yards of him and he missed the ball completely. It bounced off his shoulder, to be pounced on by a thankful Walsall defence."

When Walsall scored early in the second half, the resulting cheer was heard two miles away. The 2-0 defeat was made certain when Gunners left back, Tommy Black, upended Walsall striker, Gilbert Allsop, to concede a penalty. Black was transfer-listed immediately after the game by Chapman - "His foul was undoubtedly the result of provocation," remarked Bastin, "but Mr Chapman would not suffer behaviour like that from any player at Highbury."

Many football clichés have had long lives and Bastin was able to coin another, when he attempted to draw some solace from the defeat. "As it was," he wrote, "we were left to concentrate on the league and eventually carried it off with several points to spare. That was certainly some consolation but the Walsall defeat still rankles in my mind. I believe it always will."

Bastin was correct - his side concentrated on the league. Arsenal won five times in succession in April and ran out four points ahead of Aston Villa, to claim the 1932/33 Division One title with 58 points.

Arsenal the Innovators

It was not just that Herbert Chapman was a great tactician - he also persuaded the club to try out new ideas and develop things which these days we would regard as commonplace in football.

One of his earliest moves was to introduce numbered shirts, which were worn for the first time in the league on 25 August 1928, by Arsenal, who played at Sheffield Wednesday and on the same day, by Chelsea, who entertained Swansea at Stamford Bridge. Chapman also had a 12ft diameter, 45-minute clock erected on top of the North Bank - though, when the FA objected, its markings were changed to those of a standard clock.

The manager had other plans. He advocated, for example, the use of floodlights and after being impressed by what he had seen on the continent, he had them built into the West Stand. However, the FA had them banned, because they feared that if the idea caught on, "clubs would be drawn into spending too much money." But in 1951, manager Tom Whittaker, who had been trainer under Chapman, put on a literally brilliant show, when Arsenal defeated the Hapoel club of Tel Aviv 6-1 in front of 44,000, in a friendly match.

Shedding light for the benefit of the paying public was one thing - bringing football to people at home through radio broadcasts was another thing Arsenal helped to pioneer during this period. The first football match broadcast on radio was the Arsenal-Sheffield United league game on 22 January 1927. An announcer - who just happened to be one George Allison - gave a running commentary, while his colleague called out numbers referring to sections on the pitch, to help listeners follow play on a simple chart, a device which helped the commentators coin the phrase, "So it's back to square one."

Then there was Gillespie Road, the local station on the London Underground, which was named in honour of Arsenal in 1932. This amazing publicity stunt was engineered by Chapman, who was eager to exploit any means of advertising the club's presence.

Right at the end of the triumphant thirties, the last competitive game at Highbury before the Second World War was played against Brentford in May 1939. Arsenal won 2-0, with goals from Alf Kirchen and Ted Drake but the match was more notable for the fact that it was used as the backdrop for a film, *The Arsenal Stadium Mystery.*

The story centred around a footballer who died by poisoning during a game. Scotland Yard investigated and all the Arsenal and 'Trojan' players come under suspicion. The film provided some wonderful footage of the great pre-war Arsenal team, both on and off the pitch, showing ground, dressing rooms and other behind-the-scenes views of the East Stand.

Brentford, in an unusual change strip, played the fictional part of 'The Trojans' and several Arsenal personalities took part in the film, including Cliff Bastin, Tom Whittaker and George Allison.

The film came after Chapman's death. But the Arsenal colours that appeared in it had been determined six years earlier, when in March 1933, Chapman added the white sleeves to the Gunners red top for a home match with Liverpool. Just another one of those little things that made the Arsenal name and image so recognisable around the world.

Death in the Family

With the Gunners at the height of their powers, in the midst, as it turned out, of three successive League Championship triumphs, Herbert Chapman's untimely death in January 1933 brought great sadness to Highbury.

Chapman's end came when it was least expected. He had caught a chill during a game at Bury on New Year's Day 1934 but visited Sheffield to watch Wednesday the following day, because Arsenal were due to meet them soon. Then, with a temperature and against doctor's orders the manager watched a third team game in the bitter cold at Guildford. Pneumonia set in and Chapman died. The news came on the morning of Arsenal's home game with Wednesday on 6 January and players and fans learned of it from newspaper billboards as they made their way to the ground.

The funeral four days later befitted a king. A vast crowd lined the street to watch the cortege, draped in red and white, move from Chapman's home in Haslemere Avenue to Hendon Parish Church. Cars, coaches and lorries brought more than 240 wreaths, most in red and white, while the pall-bearers numbered some of Arsenal's greatest players - Jack, Bastin, Lambert, Hulme, Hapgood and James.

The sadness even evoked poetry, inspiring 'The Lost Captain', by Thomas Moult:

> The last whistle has sounded, the great game is over.
> O, was ever a field left so silent as this;
> The scene a bright hour since, how empty it is;
> What desolate splendour the shadows now cover,
> The captain has gone. The splendour was his.

Chapman was to be commemorated in the marble bust by Jacob Epstein, which stands in the club's entrance hall. Also preserved at Highbury is his carved chapel seat, given to the club by his church in Yorkshire in 1931. More than that, some denizens of Highbury will tell you that Chapman's ghost still haunts the corridors of the stadium.

Chapman's funeral.

Continuity

Chapman's death posed an awkward problem for Arsenal's directors, the task of finding a suitable successor. For the first few months, they took the expedient route, allowing reserve team manager, Joe Shaw, to run the team with overall management duties handled by George Allison. Shaw duly guided the side to a second successive Championship but in June, Allison was appointed secretary-manager of the club.

He had come by a circuitous route to the job. In 1903, at the age of 20 he began work as a reporter on Teesside, covering local games, before he became assistant to the secretary-manager at Middlesbrough. In 1906 he moved to London and returned to journalism, where after years of reporting Woolwich Arsenal matches from Plumstead, he found he had a strong affinity for the club.

Once in place, he took his chance: Allison was to guide the club to two League Championships and the FA Cup before war broke out and completed the third leg of three straight title wins the following season.

That first season under the new manager saw a new star in the making and one Allison could call his own. Ted Drake, from Southampton, the manager's first signing, scored a club record 42 goals in his first season at Highbury, claiming a hat-trick on no less than seven occasions. That autumn, the first four home games produced 21 Arsenal goals, including eight against Liverpool. The season concluded memorably, too, when Arsenal's injured keeper, Frank Moss, playing on for nuisance value down the wing, scored a stunning goal at Goodison Park to virtually tie up the title for the Gunners.

Seven-Goal Hero

The seasons that followed, if not as glorious, were good by any standards: sixth, third, first and fifth in the league - and FA Cup winners in 1936. That less-than-pulsating victory over Sheffield United was decided by a single goal from Ted Drake, who had earlier in the season notched an even more notable feat, when he scored all seven goals against Aston Villa in a league fixture in Birmingham.

Those at the game noted that it was Villa who began the game brightly and there was no hint of the troubles ahead for them. Early on, indeed, Drake skidded on the pitch and fell flat on his face, to the amusement of the home support. The fun, however, started for Arsenal and their centre forward after 15 minutes. Moving out to the left to collect a pass from Pat Beasley, Drake pushed the ball through the legs of Welshman Tommy Griffiths and ran on to collect the ball and shoot through the legs of goalkeeper, Harry Morton. Then, after a mazy run by Bastin, Drake added a second when a pass from the winger left him clear. He shrugged off challenges from Griffiths and George Cummings before smashing the ball past the helpless Morton. Drake then secured a first-half hat-trick, when a shot from Beasley rebounded from a defender to leave him with an open goal.

Early in the second half, the crowd sensed that something special was happening. Within five minutes of the break, the centre forward had added two more goals - the first taking advantage of careless defending by the hapless Griffiths, the second after he was fed by Bastin again. Then, on 58 minutes, he hit his sixth shot on goal from the edge of the box - and claimed his sixth goal.

By this time the whole Villa defence had taken to marking Drake but they were still unable to stop him crashing another shot against the underside of the bar, which eventually was cleared. However, in the 89th minute, he struck again, finding enough room to take yet another Bastin pass, before cracking it home.

Arsenal trainer, Tom Whittaker, described the atmosphere in the dressing room after this virtuoso performance:

"I well remember, during the laughter and excitement in our dressing room after the game over our young centre forward's tremendous feat, the Villa players Danny Blair, George Cummings and Alex Massie coming in with the ball which had been used for the match. On it were the signatures of the Villa team. And Massie said: 'For you Ted - and there's no hard feelings'. The perfect gesture on the perfect day."

It could have been worse for the home side, too - Drake was not fully fit and was playing with his knee strapped up after suffering a niggling strain for some weeks. And Alex James was missing from the team altogether. Lucky Villa.

Ted Drake, who scored 42 goals in 41 games in 1934/35.

End of An Era

No-one could gainsay Allison's achievements in the latter part of the 1930s - the side battled to yet another Championship in 1937/38 - but Arsenal had peaked in the heyday of Alex James on the park and Herbert Chapman off it. James' retirement in 1937 coincided with that of Bob John and though Arsenal, with tactical shifts and expensive purchases, attempted to replace the Scot, they were never to succeed.

Allison finally broke the bank in August 1938 seeking the magic replacement, when he paid £14,000, another British record, to Wolves for Bryn Jones. The move hardly had time to prove itself but Jones' first season at Highbury was not a happy one and though he emerged again to play for the Gunners for three seasons after the war, Jones could never replace one of British football's greats. But then, who could?

Triumphs of the 1930s:

1930/31 Championship

Arsenal became the first southern side to win the league. They scored 127 goals and with 66 points, set a new record to clinch the title.

1932/33 Championship

As the season drew to a close, Arsenal won five games in succession, clinching the title with a 3-1 win over Chelsea at Stamford Bridge.

1933/34 Championship

The Gunners claimed the title, defeating their closest rivals, Huddersfield Town and Derby County, in successive matches over a memorable Easter.

1934/35 Championship

Arsenal won the title for the third successive season. Ted Drake marked his first Gunners campaign by scoring 42 goals for the club.

1936 FA Cup

Despite an injury crisis, Arsenal captured the FA Cup, defeating Sheffield United 1-0 in the final.

1937/38 Championship

Arsenal amassed only 52 points - their lowest in any Championship season in the 1930s - but despite 11 defeats, the Gunners were still good enough to win the title.

Arsenal Managers, 1925-1947:

Herbert Chapman, 1925-1934

George Allison, 1934-1947

The Nearly Years

The Tradition Lives On

During the war, George Allison practically ran Arsenal on his own for seven years, helping to organise the friendlies and cup ties that kept some semblance of normality around Highbury during the dreadful years of the Blitz and the Second World War.

No-one could question that Allison gave his all for the club, or that he always had the best interests of Arsenal at heart but he was more of a figurehead than his predecessor, Herbert Chapman, without his mentor's football brain. Rather than Allison, Tom Whittaker and Joe Shaw took over much of the management of the players. The first season back in action after the war, 1946/47, was a poor one for the Gunners and only a late run of victories - inspired by new signings, the veterans Ronnie Rooke and Joe Mercer - finally buried fears of relegation, with the club finishing 13th in the First Division. Despite his long involvement with the club, the secretary-manager decided it was time to retire.

Tom Whittaker, a former Arsenal player, whose career had been blighted by injury, was Allison's natural replacement. He had already built up a reputation as the finest trainer in the game, not only to Arsenal in the most successful era, the late 1920s and 1930s but also to the England team and with touring FA teams, with whom he had travelled all over the world.

After he was demobilised in 1946, Whittaker had been appointed assistant manager to Allison and his succession followed a year later. Almost immediately, he effected an extraordinary transformation at Highbury, signing Don Roper from Southampton and the Scot, Archie MacAulay, from Brentford and moulding a team that won the First Division the very next season, his first as manager.

It was a triumph built around the goals of Ronnie Rooke, who was the First Division's top scorer. An unlikely signing from Fulham at the age of 35 for £1,000, he had already scored 21 goals from 24 games in the season immediately after the war. The following year brought still greater success, as Rooke netted 33 times, including four in the final match of the season at home to Grimsby Town. By then, Arsenal were home and dry - they had secured the title with a draw at Huddersfield, with four games of the season still remaining.

Joe Mercer, at 32, converted from an attacking to a defensive wing half when he moved to Arsenal. As captain, he was to play as important a role as Rooke, marshalling what he called a 'retreating defence' - a tactic we might recognise today. If the ball was lost, rather than plunge directly into a tackle, Mercer, with MacAulay alongside him, preferred to back away from the opposition and instead pack the centre of defence. It wasn't necessarily a crowd-pleasing tactic, nor did it draw applause from the press but it proved almost infallible against their opponents, most of whom were unable to contrive a way round it.

The manager's success continued in 1950, when he guided Arsenal to an FA Cup Final. It was a remarkable run for the Gunners, who played every one of their cup ties in London. The most exciting of these was against Chelsea in the semi final, when, with five minutes to go and trailing 2-1, centre half Leslie Compton ignored Mercer's orders and went up for a corner, taken by his brother Denis. He headed a powerful equaliser to complete a glorious comeback, for Chelsea had led 2-0. Freddie Cox, it was, who scored the decisive goal for the Gunners in the replay.

At Wembley, Arsenal always had the edge over a strong Liverpool side. Their half back line Leslie Compton, the inspirational Mercer and the fiery dynamo, Alex Forbes, was outstanding. In inside-right, Jimmy Logie, they had the man of the match and their young striker Peter Goring, proved a handful for the Liverpool defence. It was Logie who produced the perfect through pass for Reg Lewis to score after 18 minutes. Lewis, a clinical finisher, got his second on 63 minutes after a Denis Compton cross had been touched on by Cox.

With rain pouring down, Liverpool battled back but they faced an impervious and ancient Arsenal defence - none would see 30 again - and even with the inspirational Billy Liddell firing against them, the Gunners held on for their third FA Cup win.

The game was remarkable, too, for it was billed as Denis Compton's swansong for the club. At 32 and after 59 league and cup games, Compton junior had decided to concentrate on his flourishing cricket career. An indifferent first half at Wembley, was followed by a thoughtful team talk from Allison, who told Compton: "Now - you have 45 minutes left of your soccer career. I want you to go out there and give it every ounce you possibly can." As well as this verbal sustenance, Compton downed a glass of whisky for courage and went out to play a full part in Arsenal's dogged second half display.

There was more glory for the brothers Compton in October, when brother Leslie was given an England debut - at the tender age of 38.

Under Allison's guidance, Arsenal maintained their status as one of the country's leading sides. A poor run after Christmas put paid to thoughts of a league title in 1950/51 but the following season, the Gunners came within two victories of stealing the Championship from Manchester United. A long league campaign, however, combined with a battling cup run, took its toll on the side and by late in the season, the squad was hard hit by injuries. And so, after once again defeating London rivals, Chelsea, in a semi final replay, Arsenal were at Wembley. The Gunners went into the game weakened by injury. Jimmy Logie played in midfield although he had been hospitalised earlier in the week, while centre half, Ray Daniel turned out with a broken wrist. Then, with only 25 minutes gone, fullback Walley Barnes, twisted his knee so badly that he was obliged to leave the field. With no substitutes allowed, Arsenal were faced with playing the remainder of the game with just 10 men.

Arsenal battled heroically in defence and attack and with just 11 minutes left, a header from centre forward, Doug Lishman, skimmed the bar, when the whole of Highbury thought a goal was certain. But just five minutes later, Arsenal were undone. With Holton and Roper both down injured, skipper Mercer yelled at referee, Arthur Ellis, to stop the play and allow treatment for the players. The ball, however, was still in play and Mitchell was allowed to cross for George Robledo to head home off the post. Arsenal still came back and had enough time to hit the bar - but the victory went to the Geordies, their last at Wembley.

Later, Mercer, addressing a celebration banquet, said: "I thought football's greatest honour was to captain England. I was wrong. It was to captain Arsenal today."

Perhaps the team spirit forged over the years and proved at Wembley, was the key. But with an ageing side, Allison's Arsenal proved good enough to claim another Championship - the club's seventh - the following season. It was a season that went down to the wire, with Arsenal and Preston North End scrapping for victory over the last weeks of the season.

North End won their final game, 1-0 at bottom club, Derby County, leaving Arsenal to meet Burnley at home and needing victory to take the title. Over 51,000 people poured into Highbury for that game. The Clarets, in the top six of the First Division, started in a business-like way and after eight minutes they took the lead, when a shot was deflected past Swindin by Mercer. However, within a minute, Alex Forbes had equalised. Thereafter, Arsenal attacked and two fine moves, converted by Doug Lishman and Jimmy Logie appeared to have put Arsenal in the clear.

Burnley, though, fought back strongly in the second half and pulled a goal back with 16 minutes to go. The final minutes seemed to last for hours, as the Lancashire side laid siege to the Arsenal goal but Arsenal, aided by some fine goalkeeping by George Swindin, held on to claim the title on goal average - by 0.099 of a goal.

Joe Mercer is held aloft with the FA Cup after Arsenal defeated Liverpool 2-0 at Wembley in 1950.

Slow Burn

The final game of the 1952/53 season, however, had been a turning point for Arsenal, as one team passed into history. The Gunners started the next season calamitously, losing six and drawing two of their first eight games. True, some players came back from injury, and the attack was strengthened when the 34-year-old Tommy Lawton signed but at best, this was a transitional period, which proved a marked contrast to the earlier glory days of Cups and Championships.

The lack of success distressed Whittaker and he was finally ordered to take a complete rest from the game. He was found to be suffering from nervous exhaustion and entered hospital. A short while later, in October 1956, he died of a heart attack.

It was the end of an era for the club, as links with Herbert Chapman's management were lost and Arsenal began to flounder as the modern game developed. Between 1953 and 1970, not a single trophy came to adorn the Arsenal cabinet and the side became a fixture in mid-table.

It was a period of managers who tried but failed to turn the downward trend. Former Gunners wing half, Jack Crayston, followed Allison into the job and took the Gunners to a laudable fifth in the First Division - their highest finish throughout the 17-year drought. But when, the following year, the Gunners tallied their lowest points total since 1930, Crayston resigned, to be followed by another Arsenal player, George Swindin.

Swindin brought in new talent - Tommy Docherty and George Eastham, Laurie Brown and John MacLeod - but in a four-year reign, the former goalkeeper was unable to find the magic touch an impatient support demanded. The fact of their near-neighbours' success - Tottenham won the 'double' - hardly helped and Swindin finally resigned sad and disillusioned.

Great Games

Through a long, bleak period in the club's history, Arsenal are better remembered for some of the individual games they played rather than their form over the season.

Some - like the first match under floodlights, played between Arsenal and Hapoel of Tel Aviv - were remembered for non-footballing reasons, others for the brilliance of the games themselves. The Gunners, for example, became the first Football League club to play in Russia, when they accepted an invitation for a mid-season friendly with Dynamo Moscow. The 5-0 thrashing that resulted did little to boost confidence, as Arsenal were overrun by a superior side.

In 1958, Highbury itself witnessed perhaps the finest game seen there since the 1930s, when Manchester United emerged victors by a single goal in a nine-goal thriller, to stay at second place in the league.

The capacity 64,000 crowd gasped at the breathtaking football of the visitors early on, as they raced to a 3-0 interval lead. Duncan Edwards and Eddie Colman dominated the midfield and Ken Morgans fairly fired down the flank at the Arsenal defence. Edwards, Bobby Charlton and Tommy Taylor scored to give United a seemingly impregnable lead. Even the Arsenal fans, they say, sat back and looked forward to more magic from the Busby Babes in the second half - but instead, it was the Gunners who came out blazing. Galvanised by captain, Dave Bowen, they scored three goals in as many minutes, through David Herd and two for Jimmy Bloomfield. United hit back with goals from Dennis Viollet and Taylor, before Derek Tapscott set up a breathless finish, in which United just held on. The applause at the end was deafening for both the visitors and the Gunners, who on that glorious afternoon had almost matched them.

Five days later, the United side was virtually wiped out in the Munich air disaster.

Wrights and Wrongs

After George Swindin's departure, Billy Wright was next to take up the managerial cudgels at Highbury. In 1959, he had won his 100th England cap, in a victory over Scotland, after playing for Wolves the length of his career. Not surprisingly, with his fame, he came to Arsenal in a blaze of publicity and the immediate purchase of Anglo-Scottish forward, Joe Baker, from Torino for £70,000, gave a promise of good times to come.

Baker brought with him some improvement - the Arsenal forward line knocked home 86 goals in his first season but the defence let in almost as many, as Arsenal finished a respectable seventh in the table. The following year, they were eighth. But despite the signing of Scot, Ian Ure and the later acquisition of Frank McLintock from Leicester City for £80,000, Wright was unable to take Arsenal up to the higher plane that Highbury demanded. On the contrary, the club faltered - 14th in the league and knocked out in the third round of the cup by struggling Blackburn Rovers. It got worse. On 5 May 1966, for a home match with Leeds, Highbury housed a crowd of just 4,554.

By then, the Gunners - the directors and the fans alike - had become impatient for success. They had tried and tested coaches from within the club; with Wright, they had experimented with an outsider. Who could they turn to now? Their physiotherapist, of course.

Arsenal Managers, 1947-1966:

Tom Whittaker, 1947-1956

Jack Crayston, 1956-1958

George Swindin, 1958-1962

Billy Wright, 1962-1966

England's most capped player of his day, Billy Wright, took his first job in management at Arsenal. Things started badly - he put the paper in his typewriter the wrong way round.

Cups and Double

Bertie Mee, the surprise choice for the manager's job in 1966, achieved within five years, a success that even the great Herbert Chapman had been unable to pull off, when he led Arsenal to the 'double'.

Mee had been a talented player in his youth and had a brief career with Derby County and Mansfield Town, sadly cut short by injury. After six years' service in the Royal Army Medical Corps, he qualified as a physiotherapist and spent 12 years working in a difficult and challenging job as a rehabilitation officer for disabled servicemen. He had, however, remained closely associated with football through FA training courses and was a familiar figure to most coaches and managers in the game, when, in August 1960, he became Arsenal's trainer and physiotherapist.

Once he had taken the reins, Mee moved quickly to strengthen the Gunners' squad. At the end of his first season, he had signed Bob McNab from Huddersfield, George Graham from Chelsea and Colin Addison from Nottingham Forest and led a recovery in league form that resulted in seventh position in the table.

The following season, as if to herald the club's re-emergence, his Arsenal side fought their way through to a Wembley appearance in the League Cup Final with Leeds. It was, however, by no means a classic, one reporter calling it, "a dreadful, impoverished game." The winning Leeds goal, scored by Terry Cooper, was decidedly dubious, after their centre half, Jack Charlton, had impeded goalkeeper, Jim Furnell but thereafter, Arsenal struggled to battle back. As it turned out, Mee's side and the Leeds team, under Don Revie, were developing into the dominant forces of the period and this dour tussle was indicative of some of the hard games that would be fought out between them over the coming seasons.

The next year, Arsenal were at Wembley again, in the same competition. Their opponents this time were Third Division Swindon Town, who had reached the final, having beaten Burnley at the third attempt at the semi-final stage.

Many of the Highbury side came into that Wembley game suffering from the after effects of a flu bug and though they dominated much of the game in normal time, the effects of the illness - combined with very heavy conditions at Wembley - appeared to have sapped them of the energy needed to cope with the extra period, after the Gunners' Bobby Gould had found a late equaliser to Roger Smart's first-half goal for the Third Division side.

In the cloying mud of Wembley, many of the Arsenal players were simply unfit for 30 more minutes. Swindon seized their chance and after 15 minutes, Don Rogers poked them into the lead. Then in the second period, Rogers sealed his place in Wembley folklore, running from half way to score a wonderful solo goal and seal victory for the underdogs.

It was a shattering blow to morale but Mee and his coach, Don Howe, rallied the players to their best league position - fourth - since 1953 and a place in Europe.

Bertie Mee, physiotherapist and manager of Arsenal.

Victory in Europe

So, at last, another major honour arrived at Highbury, when, against all odds, the Gunners claimed the European Fairs Cup - which is today known as the UEFA Cup.

It was Arsenal's home form that was the key to the club's success, particularly against two giants from the Low Countries - Ajax and Anderlect - and against Sporting Lisbon. Their triumph was built on Bertie Mee's home-grown, humdrum squad of players, for whom teenager, Eddie Kelly, the indomitable George Armstrong and local-boy-made-good, Charlie George, all shone.

As ever in European competition, the route to the final was long and hard. A 3-1 aggregate victory over Glentoran in the first round owed much to the skills of George Graham, who scored two headed goals, effectively to end the tie in the 3-0 first leg win at Highbury.

In the second round, the Gunners played impressively to hold Sporting Lisbon to a goalless draw in the away leg. Arsenal defended coolly and could count on goalkeeper Geoff Barnett, who saved a Peres penalty after Peter Simpson had fouled Marinho. The priority now was a home win. This, they achieved with ease. Though Marinho hit the Arsenal bar in the first half, it was Arsenal who threatened, pressing their visitors back and finding ample space to launch their assaults. They took the lead when a central defender clumsily miskicked a cross to John Radford, who had time to control the ball and shoot home. Graham made it two with another header before half time and then, after the break, the Scot got a touch on a fierce Bob McNab drive to put the tie beyond doubt.

Faced with Rouen, Arsenal played their away fixture in the first leg cautiously and defensively - an approach adopted by their French opponents in the return leg at Highbury. When Jon Sammels knocked home a headed flick from Charlie George in the 179th minute of play, the cheer might almost have been one of relief from a crowd which would not be faced with the purgatory of extra time. The only other incident was a fine save by the Rouen goalkeeper Rigoni, who stopped a fierce volley from Peter Marinello. The Scot was making his home debut after his £100,000 move from Hibernian.

Next up were Baku Dynamo of Rumania - who set Arsenal an easy enough task in the away half of the tie. Arsenal took the lead after 57 minutes, when George shot against the underside of the bar from Storey's pass and Sammels hit home the rebound. After 80 minutes, McNab's centre was calmly converted by Radford.

The second leg was won at a canter, as Baku, conquerors of Kilmarnock earlier in the competition, proved almost unworthy opponents for this stage of the competition. Arsenal, with Eddie Kelly irresistible in midfield, were having a party. They scored seven with ease and long before the final whistle, the North Bank were chanting, "We want ten!" The goals came from Radford, Sammels and George, who each scored two, and from Graham.

The Gunners were almost there but were faced in the semi-finals by the famous Ajax of Amsterdam. By this late stage in the season, the Dutch held no terrors for Bertie Mee's side, who by now had found the rhythm that would be so richly rewarded over the next year and more. They, quite simply, thrashed their challengers in the first leg.

That said, it seemed for a long period that the Gunners would be limited to a single goal, scored by George after McNab's cross was headed out. With a young Johan Cruyff hovering on the wing, Arsenal had to be wary of the counter attack and it took till late in the game for the home side to really exploit their advantage. Finally, the Ajax defence wilted with 12 minutes to go. Sammels was left unmarked for Armstrong's centre and while his first shot was blocked by the goalkeeper, Bals, his second flew home. Then, moments later, Graham won a penalty, which George scored with relish. It was an inspiring night for Arsenal, for the players and fans and for Mee, who saw youngsters such as George and Kelly more than hold their own against one of the best sides in Europe, while in centre forward Radford, the manager was blessed with a player who simply never knew when to stop running.

In Amsterdam, Arsenal played as defensively as Ajax had at Highbury - but to far better effect, keeping the Dutchmen to a single goal, scored by Muhren.

And so to the first leg of the final, played in Brussels, where Anderlect proved too strong for their visitors and were inspired by their international midfielder, Paul Van Himst. For much of the game, they ran the show and Arsenal were indebted to their goalkeeper, Bob Wilson, for a string of saves that kept the score to a respectable 3-0, the Belgians scoring through Devrindt and Mulder, who hit two. Then, with five minutes to go, Ray Kennedy, 18 and on as a substitute for Charlie George, connected beautifully with a George Armstrong cross to head home the goal that was a lifeline for the Gunners.

It had seemed so unpromising - yet, the second leg was to prove a completely different story. True, Anderlecht gave as good as they got for the first 25 minutes but as the game progressed, the weakness of their goalkeeper, Trappeniers, became clear. Then, on 26 minutes, Kelly collected the ball just outside the crowded penalty area, flicked it from his left foot to his right and shot powerfully wide of the static goalkeeper.

The second half followed a similar pattern to the first, with Arsenal pressing but Anderlecht threatening on the break. The visitors hit the post, before Graham sent McNab away down the left and a perfect cross was met powerfully by Radford, who headed the sides level on aggregate. Within a minute, George had swept a long ball from the left across the goal to the unmarked Sammels, who drove a low cross-shot past the goalkeeper and into the net.

Arsenal had won. And at the final whistle there was the sight of players, bare-chested in the cold, cold rain, being carried around the pitch by their ecstatic fans.

"That was probably the greatest emotional experience of my life," Mee said afterwards. "To be manager of a great club when they win a European trophy for the first time and to have my own boys win, as opposed to being lumbered with the names from the past - it was a wonderful experience."

One of Mee's stalwarts - Bob Wilson.

Arsenal at the Double

Even greater triumph was to follow for Mee and his home-spun side. Only one club - the club's great rivals, Tottenham - had achieved a 'double' of League and FA Cup in the 20th century. Arsenal were to emulate the achievement in 1970/71.

This wasn't the work of an Arsenal side bristling with international stars. The success was based on teamwork, discipline and character. Despite being six points behind Leeds United at the end of March, they displayed both the resilience and ability to pick their way past any obstacle on their way to triumph in the end.

Leeds had set the early pace in Division One but it was Arsenal who announced themselves as the No 1 contenders for the title, when they ended the Yorkshire side's perfect start to the season, holding them to a 0-0 draw at Highbury in their sixth game. Thereafter, it was nip and tuck' but after Arsenal had suffered a crushing 5-0 defeat at Stoke in late September, the Gunners embarked on a run of 14 games without defeat, drawing just three games, until they lost at Huddersfield in January. They lost twice again in their next four games - seemingly surrendering too much to their Yorkshire rivals.

But from there on, Arsenal turned the screw, winning nine successive matches, inspired by manager Mee early in the New Year:

"I told the players we could expect two matches a week for the rest of the season. As this is the case, now is the time for you to be really ambitious and to aim for the success that may never be possible for you as players again in your lifetimes," said Mee, looking back on the season. "They owed it to themselves and their colleagues to accept the challenge of the next three months."

As the season unfolded, two crucial games appeared to seal Arsenal's destiny. The first came on the last weekend of March, when Stoke City were pitted against the Gunners in the FA Cup semi final. Leading by two goals from the 30th minute, the Potteries side were pegged back in the second half by a Peter Storey drive. But an excellent Stoke side refused to sit back on their lead and continued to drive Arsenal into defence.

Salvation for the Gunners came only in injury time, when Frank McLintock thudded an Armstrong corner towards the goal, only to be denied by the outstretched hand of Stoke midfielder, John Mahoney. The delight of the Arsenal players at the penalty award was obvious still, Storey had to hammer it home, no easy task as the player testified afterwards: "The lads were all hugging each other as though we'd scored. But I was the one who had to stick it in. And past Gordon Banks too!" But he did - and the replay, a less agonising affair, was decided by goals from George Graham in the first half and Ray Kennedy. The other vital game in that 'double' season did not feature Arsenal at all but was played in mid- April at Elland Road between Leeds and West Bromwich Albion. With Albion a goal up, the game was decided in their favour by a controversial second. Tony Brown blocked a pass from Norman Hunter of Leeds and followed the ball as it rebounded into the Leeds half. The linesman flagged because Albion's Colin Suggett was in an offside position but the referee decided he was not interfering with play and allowed Brown to continue. He did so - before releasing Jeff Astle to score at his leisure. It wasn't clear-cut and many referees would have blown for offside - but Leeds and their fans were outraged and disappointed and the ensuing riot brought a fine and a ban from playing their early games at home the following season. Arsenal, meanwhile, defeated Newcastle and moved ahead of Leeds on goal average, with two games in hand.

And so to White Hart Lane. Of all places for Arsenal to win the league, if it was not to be Highbury, surely this would have been the place Arsenal fans would have chosen to do the job. Leeds had finished their games and the Gunners knew that a goalless draw against Spurs would secure their eighth Championship on goal average.

The match was played before a capacity crowd of 51,992, with a further 20,000 locked out of the ground and it was another nail-biting affair for Arsenal fans. The side did not go on the defensive against their third-placed opponents, however, and had marginally the better of a fast and exciting game. Two minutes from time, Ray Kennedy headed them into the lead - but that could have been Arsenal's undoing had Spurs equalised, the mathematics in that case awarding Leeds the title on goal average. It needed all Bob Wilson's courage in the dying seconds to dive into a forest of legs and grab the ball as Spurs threatened to score.

Afterwards, an elated Bertie Mee paid tribute to the professionalism of his young side and their ability to withstand the tests which had been presented to them:

"We don't know what the word 'pressure' means. People use the term very glibly but we have never accepted that there is such a word as 'pressure'. We're busy, yes, we like to be busy but we don't know what the words 'pressure' or 'tension' mean. We've refused to accept there *are* such things."

For goalkeeper Bob Wilson, there was simply a feeling of delight. "I enjoyed every minute of it," he said. "I made up my mind as regards to goalkeeping that I would just go for everything. I went out and enjoyed the whole evening. There were two moments when Spurs might have scored. Martin Peters hit an incredible shot on the run, which landed on top of the net. The other was a superb ball across the six-yard box and Alan Gilzean came shooting in but thankfully didn't get a foot to it.

"But really, after that, I thought, 'At least we're going to draw 0-0.' But then the climax, with that goal - that's how we wanted to win it. We didn't want goal average and 0.001, we wanted a point ahead of Leeds, so that we'd won it fair and square." As for White Hart Lane, "It was," said Wilson "a marvellous place to win the Championship"

With the Cup Final looming, Wilson offered a prediction in his post-match interview, saying of their historic league win, "I think it's worth a goal start to us."

Perhaps not quite that - but Arsenal were the stronger side throughout the final. That the event should offer so many twists, was hardly surprising in a season that had been so dramatic. In truth, the Gunners made enough chances to have won the game comfortably within 90 minutes but it had gone into extra time, when Steve Heighway broke away on the left and beat Wilson with a shot to his near post to put Liverpool a goal up.

After the game, Mee recalled the mood when that blow was struck. "I was despondent for two minutes and I know the boys were," he said. "But I perked up and I know on the field they perked each other up. They said, 'Come on, we've been down before; we can come back, we can do it again' – and lo and behold, they did do it again. You're always in with a chance when you've got this sort of attitude."

So it was to prove. Despite Liverpool's defensive record - they had only conceded 25 goals in league and FA Cup all season - Arsenal refused to panic. It was Eddie Kelly, who had come on in the second half for the injured Peter Storey, who took advantage of a rare defensive lapse to push the ball goalwards and George Graham, the man of the match, who turned to claim the goal. But whoever scored, it was Arsenal's equaliser, just before the end of the first 15 minutes.

Then, though sapped with fatigue and with eight minutes left, Charlie George hit a thunderous shot to win the game and all the honours.

"They have had a great season," acknowledged the manager in the first flush of victory. "What a tremendous side, what character and strength of character within the side today. They really showed all their best qualities."

It was an amazing performance by all of the players. Wilson and George Armstrong had played in all 64 games over the season, Frank McLintock, Ray Kennedy and Pat Rice all but one. England internationals, John Radford, Bob McNab and Peter Storey missed all but two. You might call it a settled side.

For Mee, an ambition remained: "I wanted to win the Cup for Frank McLintock. The League Championship was for my chairman, Denis Hill-Wood. For myself? I wouldn't mind the European Cup next season. I know we have done the 'double', but at the moment it is too much to take in."

Frank McLintock and Charlie George celebrate the 'double'.

Wilderness Years

The ambition, the expectation and the fine talk of the 'double' year was never fulfilled by Bertie Mee's Arsenal side and though they performed well enough the following season, the fortunes of the club began to ebb.

After a disastrous start - three defeats in August - the 1971/72 season brought a creditable fifth place in the league in the final analysis. The European Cup, the trophy Mee had set his sights on, proved elusive, with the Gunners quitting the competition in the quarter finals, having lost home and away to Ajax of Amsterdam, Europe's dominant side at the time and on their way to the second of three successive European Cup wins.

Only in the FA Cup did Arsenal make any real headway, though it was a stuttering, difficult run. Away fixtures at Swindon and Reading proved tough enough obstacles, before a cup tie against Champions-to-be, Derby and their manager, Brian Clough. After a 2-2 draw at the Baseball Ground, a crowd of 63,077 packed into Highbury for the goalless replay. Finally at Filbert Street, a neutral venue, Ray Kennedy decided the tie in the Gunners' favour. A victory over Orient then set up another semi final with Stoke. Again, it was desperately close and again a replay was required - and this time Charlie George and John Radford booked Arsenal's passage.

The Centenary Cup Final, against increasingly bitter rivals Leeds, was a hard game, with a foul in the first seconds and a booking - for Arsenal's Bob McNab - inside the first two minutes.

Arsenal had their chances in the game. David Harvey, preferred in the Leeds goal to Gary Sprake, saved well from Frank McLintock, Paul Reaney kicked Alan Ball's superb volley off the line; and Charlie George hit the bar in the second half. For all that, the Gunners were never as creative as their opponents, who subsequently were to come within a point of winning the league. Allan Clarke hit the bar, before he stooped to head powerfully past Geoff Barnett after a cross from Mick Jones. He might have had a second, had Gray found him late on in the game and Arsenal finished well beaten.

Other managers had faced the problem - but Mee had been battling to stop his side from breaking up. Coach, Don Howe, had left after the 'double' success. Now veterans such as Frank McLintock , Peter Storey and Peter Simpson were coming to the end of their playing careers. Others, like Charlie George and Ray Kennedy moved on and Arsenal's abilities and collective presence were reduced. At the end of the 1974/75 season, they finished 16th. The following season, it was a place worse. Finally, Mee announced that he would quit.

Cups of Cheer?

It has been done since but it was Terry Neill who became the first person to have managed both of the two big North London clubs, Arsenal and Spurs. A former Gunners player, his track record in management at White Hart Lane was not overly impressive but his initial gesture on his return to Highbury was reassuring - he signed England's most exciting centre forward, Malcolm MacDonald, from Newcastle for £333,333.

The first season brought an improvement in the club's league showing and then, with the return of Don Howe as coach, began a startling run of three FA Cup Final appearances in succession. The first, against Ipswich, was a lacklustre show by the Gunners and even the most ardent of fans might have been prepared to admit that the Suffolk side deserved their day in the sun, after Roger Osborne scored their winner late in the game.

The next year was a different story and provided a game with a finale rarely matched and never surpassed for excitement. By now, Neill had brought through talent of his own in Liam Brady, Frank Stapleton and David O'Leary and all three Irishmen were to appear in a pulsating FA Cup Final with Manchester United.

With less than five minutes left of the game, the Londoners led by two goals, from Brian Talbot and Frank Stapleton. Then, without his side ever having looked like scoring, Gordon McQueen fastened on to a Joe Jordan pass to pull United back, before Sammy McIlroy equalised - and it seemed that dispirited Arsenal were facing extra time, with and a minute a half to go.

No-one reckons with genius - and Arsenal provided it in the shape of Liam Brady. A driving run down the left and a floating cross over goalkeeper, Gary Bailey, allowed perm-headed Alan Sunderland to go down in history with a stunning last-minute winner and a much-photographed goal celebration. "It was murder, murder. But what a relief at the end of it!" breathed Neill afterwards.

Relief turned to disappointment the next season, when Arsenal lost both the FA Cup and European Cup Winners' Cup finals, in the space of four days, to West Ham and Valencia respectively. Each game brought its own bitter disappointment. The FA Cup defeat was at the hands of London rivals and to a Second Division side. In Europe, the loss was as narrow as it could have been, Arsenal becoming the first side to lose such an important game on penalties, after misses by Liam Brady and Graham Rix.

Though there had seemed to be a level of promise about the Arsenal team, there now followed seven fallow years at Highbury. Neill's regime could not stand up to the loss of key personnel, notably Brady to Italian football and Stapleton to Manchester United and despite the fact that his side never fell below tenth in the league, he was sacked in December 1983 and replaced by Don Howe. The former coach brought in new personnel, notably Paul Mariner and Viv Anderson but like Neill, he failed to achieve the high levels of success demanded by followers of the club and by the spring 1986, Howe had asked to be released from his contract.

A new figure was needed to revive a once-great club. The press was full of rumours that suggested a certain Terry Venables was Highbury-bound, a chirpy character with some interesting business deals and a flash demeanour. Instead, Arsenal hired George Graham.

Arsenal Managers 1966-1986:

Bertie Mee, 1967-1976

Terry Neill, 1976-1983

Don Howe, 1983-1986

Gentleman George

George Graham arrived at Highbury with a bigger reputation for playing than management. An integral part of the 'double'-winning side of the early seventies, even if his lackadaisical manner had resulted in the bestowing of his 'Stroller' moniker, he was to return to North London after a period in charge of Millwall. At The Den, he had performed admirably, nurturing a young, improving side, despite the constant backdrop of hooliganism that so blighted that club in the mid-eighties.

At Arsenal, he was to find a more benign group of supporters, who remembered him fondly and who, more importantly, were seeking someone, anyone, to provide a bit of glamour and spark to a side now playing in front of crowds that were regularly as low as 20,000. Most still think of Graham's time as weaving inexorably to Anfield on a famous May night in 1989 but there were other stopping places before Liverpool and some similarly memorable days since.

And then there is Graham's leaving of North London after having won the club six major trophies in eight seasons. His departure was a desolate affair after so much success and so much hard work. A press statement from chairman, Peter Hill-Wood, stating that, "Mr. Graham did not act in the best interests of the club," said all that could really be said.

Graham certainly found it hard. "After eight and a half years, they sacked me in two minutes," he complained, yet in many ways, time had already been called, at least in the stands, with fans complaining of a return to the dull Arsenal of pre-Graham times. In his third-last season, Arsenal staked the embarrassing claim to being the lowest scorers in the entire Premiership, despite being able to field Ian Wright, one of Highbury's greatest post-war forwards. Graham's era was nearing an end but how the memories live on.

George Graham changed things by not really changing things at all. At least, not initially. His methods were as subtle as his choice of suits and as devastatingly effective. He brought with him an ability to motivate and he vowed he would not rush in with thoughts of immediately making Arsenal a 'George Graham' side. Indeed, he did not buy an established player until the end of his first full season, when Alan Smith arrived from Leicester City, a particularly shrewd investment.

George Graham and the Championship trophy.

Cups of Joy and Sorrow

It was at the back that the new Arsenal began to take shape. Kenny Sansom, Viv Anderson, David O'Leary and a young Tony Adams gelled into a formidable defensive unit and an unbeaten run of 22 games saw Arsenal reach the summit of the First Division in time to celebrate their Centenary, at Christmas 1986. Two days after Christmas Day, the date of the club's formation a hundred years earlier, Graham's side played Southampton at Highbury, and the party atmosphere was made all the more joyous by the 1-0 win that kept Arsenal at the top of the league. Twenty four Gunners legends, including Joe Mercer and Ted Drake, were there on this momentous day and a suitably reverent North Bank afforded them all a noisy welcome back. Yet, how these supporters ached to cheer a sign of tangible success as well as these keepers of an old flame, and while this was not to come in the league, not yet anyway, rumours of Arsenal's re-emergence were confirmed at Wembley later that season, on a lush April day.

The Littlewoods Cup was not a trophy over-adorned with prestige but it had never before taken up residence at Highbury and was collected via an impressive run of results. Huddersfield, Manchester City, Charlton and Nottingham Forest had all been disposed of before Spurs were gleefully vanquished in the semi final. Arsenal's opponents at Wembley were Liverpool, who had already lifted the trophy four times that decade, in its previous League and Milk Cup guises. However, while this was a long way from a rump Anfield side, it was certainly a period of transition and with Kenny Dalglish on the substitute's bench and Ian Rush nearing the end of his initial spell at the club, Arsenal fans could allow themselves some splashes of optimism amid the sunshine.

However, a darkness fell in the 23rd minute, when Craig Johnston released a scampering Rush and he opened the scoring with one of his typical opportunist goals. No-one needed reminding of the fact that Liverpool had never lost when Rush scored, a run of almost 150 games, least of all those in the commentary boxes who all but wrote off Arsenal. However, few were counting on Charlie Nicholas, this under-achieving, yet still popular Scot, to steal the thunder. His two strikes either side of half time are not the best goals ever to grace Wembley but they were more than enough. His first was poked home after a scramble and his winner was even less aesthetically pleasing. After Perry Groves found him in the box, Nicholas aimed a shot at Bruce Grobbelaar but his mis-kick was rather fortuitously deflected into the net.

Many saw this cup triumph as an unexpected bonus so soon in Graham's time at the club, especially in a season so concerned with the club's past. The future was certainly looking considerably brighter than it had done just twelve months earlier but as often happens, setbacks lurked near, too.

David O'Leary

Initial signs of post-cup comedown were Tony Cottee's rejection of a move to Highbury in favour of Everton, while Charlie Nicholas could not build on his Wembley blossoming and started only three games in the 1987-88 season, before being allowed to leave for Aberdeen. It was a rather tame end to his four-year Arsenal career but he never lost the support of the fans, who remembered such gems as a 40-yard lob into the North Bank goal against Chelsea.

Despite a lack of fire power, Arsenal again made it to a second successive Littlewoods Cup Final, winning all seven games en route. This run included a fine win away to Cottee's Everton in the first leg of the semi final at Goodison Park, Groves scoring the only goal and a more resounding 3-1 victory at Highbury in the return. This was one of those great nights, when everything went right and Arsenal managed to lever their way out of some less than inspiring league form. Only four days earlier, a massive 54,161 fans had watched as Arsenal beat Manchester United in the FA Cup 5th round.

Their cup form was not to last, with Nottingham Forest halting Arsenal's FA Cup progress in the following round but worse was to come at Wembley. Unlike the year before, everything pointed to an Arsenal win in the final, for the opponents were Luton Town, a club without a trophy to its name. Another strange tale unravelled itself at Wembley, although, this time, its denouement was a long way from being scripted in North London.

As well as resounding underdogs, Luton had arrived at Wembley still reeling from a 4-1 Simod Cup Final defeat against Second Division Reading. If such a side could dismantle them, what havoc might Arsenal wreak across the wide Wembley plains? Not too much, came the answer, although Arsenal, after Mick Harford had opened the scoring for Luton with a header in the opening minutes, did have long stretches of possession and found themselves reacting to the early setback with a two-goal salvo from substitute, Martin Hayes and Alan Smith.

However, this enthralling match was a long way from finished and after Nigel Winterburn missed a penalty, his first and last for the club, an aberration by the hapless Gus Ceasar allowed Luton's Danny Wilson the chance to equalise with five minutes left. In the last minute, Brian Stein struck a winner and Arsenal fans ended an afternoon of fluctuating emotion, in numbed silence. In truth, the better side had won but this offered little consolation and neither did a league finish of sixth, 24 points behind title-winners, Liverpool.

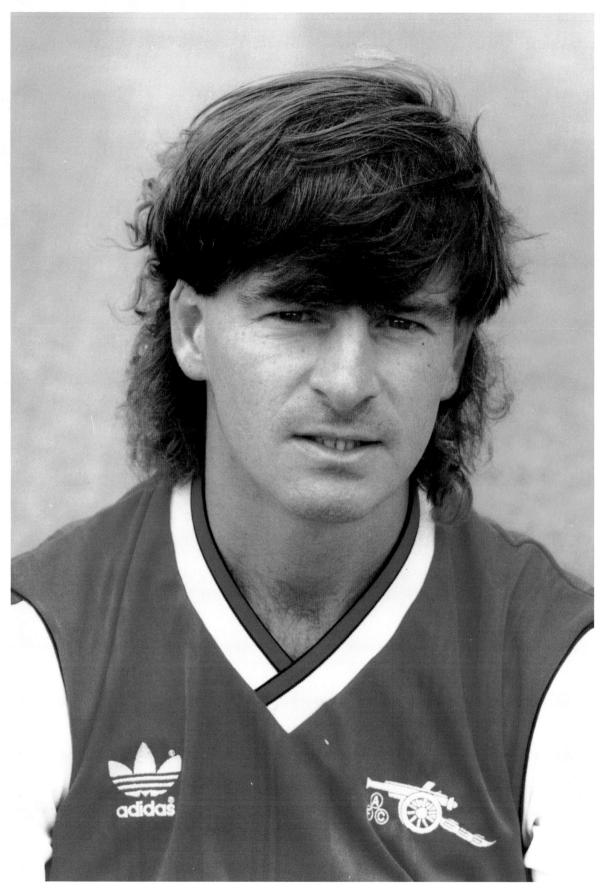

Charlie Nicholas won a League Cup Final but didn't quite fit in at Highbury.

The Ultimate Climax

The progress was continuing and if it was not immediately obvious, this was in true George Graham style. Tony Adams, Michael Thomas and Paul Merson all signed long-term contracts and signings such as Smith, Nigel Winterburn and Kevin Richardson were fitting into Graham's studious pattern of play. Disappointments such as the Luton result could only make the team stronger, a belief Graham had kept with him since his playing days.

"When I was a younger player at Aston Villa, Joe Mercer always used to say that we should treat victory and defeat with the same dignity and try to learn from them both. I'm sure we'll have gained a lot from the (cup final) experience. We're already the main force in London football. We're building a strong squad. Our ultimate aim is to win the Championship. The way we're developing, we can compete for the title next season."

And so they did, in a way so enthralling it is difficult even now, from a distance of a decade, to fully believe the drama, or imagine the trauma. The latter, of course, arrived via Hillsborough, a bleak and indelible mark across a season of such rich footballing worth, while the former waited until the last minute of the last game to fully unravel, when this taut tension found release in the right boot of Michael Thomas. It is hard to look at that season without heading straight for Anfield, to those last 60 seconds and to Thomas – but to do so would ignore other fine performers.

While Adams and O'Leary began the season looking as cohesive as a *Neighbours* storyline, the introduction of Steve Bould brought renewed solidity and these same three players switched expertly to the 'sweeper' system suddenly introduced by Graham in the spring, a move initiated after a poor 2-2 draw at home to Charlton. In midfield, David Rocastle was the creative hub, joined by Brian Marwood and at times by Michael Thomas and complemented by the steely presence of Kevin Richardson, the only member of the side with previous title winning experience from his days at Everton.

In attack, Alan Smith was, simply, Alan Smith, snaffling up priceless goals and setting up chances for others. If football was a game that did not require headlines, Smith's role in the title-deciding game on Merseyside would be as cherished as that played by Thomas. One Liverpool player remarked that you could have fired a cannonball at Smith that night and he would still have brought it down, before nudging a pass to a team-mate. This, indeed, is what he did to release Thomas for that final, thrilling run towards Grobbelaar's goal, having already scored the neat glancing header that had inched Arsenal nearer the impossible dream.

In truth, Arsenal had looked somewhat less than Championship material on several occasions in the 37 previous games. A 5-1 win against Wimbledon was as good a way to begin as any but results were often uninspiring and only twice did Arsenal manage to score more than two goals at Highbury.

That said, the team did not lose successive games during the entire season and this ability to grind out results is as much a hallmark of Champions as multi-goal thrashings. There was a spine to the side and guts too, something which could not always be said of Arsenal teams of the then recent past. How else might you account for a side travelling to face Liverpool, even a Liverpool wearied by eight games in 23 emotional post-Hillsborough days and leaving with the required 2-0 victory. It was the first time an Arsenal side had scored twice at the ground in 15 years. Bookmakers had them at 16-1 against eking out such a result but on the touchline, George Graham was harbouring something perhaps not even the most ardent Arsenal fan could honestly say they felt. He believed, he really believed.

After the final whistle sounded, he simply strode out onto Anfield and placated his giddy players, as if he felt they, too, should have expected this wondrous and outrageous result. He was then quick to add sober words to such actions, remarking that he wanted to join the Highbury Hall of Fame alongside great managers like Herbert Chapman, George Allison, Tom Whittaker and Bertie Mee. "We have laid a foundation of belief at Highbury. If you lose hope, or lose belief, you may as well get out of football. Tonight was a fairytale, the unpredictable that makes us all love football."

Arsenal players celebrate an extraordinary League Championship win.

This is Anfield - and that is Arsenal's trophy, carried off by George Graham.

Failure and Success

Not surprisingly, 1988/89 was a hard act to follow and Arsenal hardly even began scaling similarly grand heights. At the end of the next season, they finished 17 points behind Liverpool and perhaps a greater indication of the poor season suffered by a team so full of English talent, was the fact that not one player was asked to join the international squad for Italia '90. Only David O'Leary of Eire flew the Highbury flag, scoring a decisive shoot-out penalty to sink Rumania and indeed, the domestic season was probably most memorable for the defender's record-breaking 662nd Arsenal appearance in a 4-3 victory over Norwich. O'Leary even managed to produce two rare goals to celebrate, while also partaking in the mass onfield melee that resulted in a £20,000 fine for his club.

At the start of this deflating season, much was made of Graham's reluctance to add to his squad. Various reasons were given, one of the most penetrating being the lack of European challenge offered, due to the ban imposed on English clubs after Heysel and which still had another season to run. Perhaps Graham did not even believe change was needed after so rich a season. Perhaps, too, he wanted to repay his players for their perseverance, with a show of loyalty. Any complacency about the quality of the side should surely have been emphatically shattered by an embarrassing 4-1 reversal at Manchester United on the opening day of the new season. Whatever logic Graham had chosen to employ, it proved he was as fallible as anyone, something which would again be demonstrated by his eventual demise.

True to form, though, he proved he would not make the same mistake twice, and before season 1990-91, he was out scouring the market, hoping to search out some much needed fresh inspiration for his side. He paid a record fee for a goalkeeper, David Seaman, who was earning rave reports at QPR, while Anders Limpar arrived to give Highbury some of the flair that had been so lacking. And how Limpar answered the call, in a sublime season for both himself and the club. Incredibly, Arsenal were beaten only once in a league season, which, not surprisingly, yielded the club a second Championship in three years.

Not since the thirties had the club managed such a feat and it evoked hopes of the kind of decade of domination Liverpool had enjoyed in the eighties. Indeed, the Anfield club's powers were on the wane and Graeme Souness presided over a tame end to the season there, after Kenny Dalglish's shock resignation in February.

But it was the abilities of Arsenal, rather than the failings of others, for which this season will be remembered. Often, these qualities were best seen amid adversity, such as Arsenal's 3-0 demolition of Liverpool only three days after they, themselves had been torn apart 6-2 by Manchester United in the League Cup at home. In so successful a season, that result - the club's worst defeat at home for 70 years - was a temporary hitch and one that Graham admirably refused to be swayed by.

Also, Arsenal were denied their captain and inspiration, when Tony Adams was jailed for a drink driving offence, thus missing a midwinter stretch of 13 games, four of which came in a titanic FA Cup marathon with Leeds. Graham was especially distraught by his captain's spell behind bars, calling him, "my eyes and ears in the dressing room and my sergeant major on the pitch".

On top of all this, Arsenal had already been docked two points for their part in an on-field brawl with Manchester United, who, themselves, lost a point. Arsenal's impressive response to this setback was an immediate 4-0 thrashing of Southampton, telling volumes about the spirit of a side now believing the world to be pitted against them. This was not merely paranoia, with some sections of the press mounting sustained campaigns against Graham and his Gunners behaving badly. Even after that three-goal victory over Liverpool, the papers concentrated more on the controversy created by Limpar's penchant to go to ground when challenged. But it was Arsenal who had the last laugh amid all this carping and Graham to his credit, remained implacable at the heart of it all. He accepted the responsibility for the "Battle of Old Trafford" and indeed, was fined £20,000 by his own club. His players, too, got on with the job in hand. "We have this thing called resilience," he said after a draw at Spurs in January. "We won't lie down."

The only other bleak moments on the playing side to rival the heavy defeat by Manchester United, were the league capitulation at Chelsea and the FA Cup semi-final clash with Spurs. The former was the only league defeat suffered in the entire season, a record unsurpassed this century. The latter game will be forever remembered for Paul Gascoigne's audacious free kick, which sped past Seaman in the fifth minute. Although Smith dragged his side back briefly into contention, the eventual 3-1 defeat put paid to hopes of an unprecedented second 'double' success.

Again, however, this was not enough to throw the players off the title scent, despite the tears in the dressing room. Men such as Bould and the rehabilitated Adams were not prone to wilting at such testing times and this defensive department was as sound as ever, despite the change of goalkeeper behind them. Indeed, new boy, Seaman, kept an astonishing 29 clean sheets in 50 matches, although this did not surprise Graham. "When you pay the best, you get the best," he reasoned, another example of his unshakeable confidence in his players. While Souness churlishly remarked that Liverpool had thrown away the title, Alex Ferguson, of Manchester United, was rather more magnanimous. "People ask if they are worthy Champions," he said, "but they have lost only one game all season. What else must they do to prove it?" What else indeed.

The next season was, however, a rather different story. Again, Arsenal failed to offer any kind of sustained title defence and even in the much anticipated European Cup, the excitement was cut depressingly short.

Rather perversely, Graham had opted not to add to the squad, just as two years earlier in the aftermath of 1989's fabled win. A malaise had seeped in over the summer, something which not even European adventure could cure. A perfunctory dismissal of FK Austria Memphis in the first round paved the way for a meeting with Benfica. A creditable away performance, where a 1-1 draw was earned, resulted in a Highbury packed for the return. These hopes were crushed by the Brazilian, Isaias, who scored twice and ended Arsenal's European involvement in a season when many had tipped them to become the first English winners of the premier tournament since Liverpool in 1984.

Instead, Arsenal were counting the cost of being out of two cup competitions by the end of Autumn (days before the Benfica reversal, Coventry had knocked Graham's side out of the League Cup) and their scale of ambition suddenly began to diminish. It decreased further with the worst result of Graham's tenure, an FA Cup third round defeat at Wrexham. "We haven't become a bad team because of one result," was Graham's expected retort in the embarrassed aftermath but there was not just that depressing scoreline to take into account.

The Christmas and New Year period, for example, saw the gathering of just a solitary point. The one bright spot in a season that had once seemed so full of promise, was the emergence of Ian Wright. And Arsenal fans may now have learned to accept a year's lack of silver in return for this golden nugget. The striker scored 24 times in the 30 games he played after his arrival from Crystal Palace, finishing off with a significant hat-trick against Southampton, which included the last Arsenal goal celebrated by the soon-to-be-demolished North Bank.

Cup Triumphs

Despite the lack of trophy success, Arsenal had finished the season as top scorers. There was thus much to look forward to in a new era of Premiership glitz, even if the North Bank had been temporarily replaced by a mural of painted faces rather than an intimidating mass of supporters. Highbury's capacity was lowered to 29,000, which was perhaps a blessing, given some of the league football served up. Arsenal managed only 15 victories in 42 games and only eight at home. An opening day Highbury defeat by Norwich City was alarming enough, even without the four goals they scored in 45 second-half minutes. Tenth place at the season's end told its own story.

Denmark's John Jensen had been bought to add steel to the midfield, though it was creativity it badly needed. Ironically, in a time when romance seemed to have strayed so far from Highbury - the North Bank was being ripped up to be replaced by a controversial bond scheme - it was in the two domestic cup competitions that Arsenal found solace.

If their FA Cup win was a curiously underwhelming affair in terms of atmosphere - only 62,367 watched the replay win over Sheffield Wednesday - the run there had, at least, involved a deeply satisfying semi-final win over Spurs, courtesy of a Tony Adams header. And the cup-winning goal, too, was something to be cherished, especially for scorer, Andy Linighan, who, on the rare occasions he managed to make it into the starting eleven, had become used to hearing his name booed by Arsenal fans. Linighan, it was, who rose to power an injury time header into the net.

In the earlier Coca Cola Cup Final, another unlikely hero's tale had been crafted, though with an element of farce thrown in for good measure. Wednesday were also the opponents, as Arsenal attempted to win the very trophy that had begun those Graham years, six years earlier. As against Liverpool in 1987, Arsenal lost an early goal but Paul Merson equalised with a marvellous swirling shot and then set up the winner for Stephen Morrow, a hitherto unheralded piece of the Graham jig-saw.

His name was certainly well known in the days that followed and not just for his cup-winning exploits. Caught up in the excitement of the success, Tony Adams had hoisted Morrow onto his shoulders, only for the player to topple back down to terra firma, gaining a broken arm for his troubles. He was on his way to hospital before even the first of those famous 38 steps had been negotiated by a clearly upset Adams.

Never before had both domestic cups been won by the same club but this unique feat could not disguise the dismal failing in the league, the true measure of great Arsenal sides. But there was one other frontier that Graham desperately wanted to tame. After the disappointment of two seasons previously, when Benfica had so prematurely, halted Arsenal's progress in the European Cup, there was an air of unfinished business haunting the Marble Halls of Highbury.

Despite the high calibre of opposition in the Cup-Winners' Cup - Real Madrid, Ajax and holders, Parma, were all lurking ominously in the hat - Graham was presumed to have taken on board the lessons learned against Benfica. Certainly, he was a big fan of continental football and had been rich in his praise of the Lisbon giants. Now it was time for the master tactician to really show his hand and indeed, Arsenal's imperious march to the final exuded quality, as well as persistence. Odense, Standard Liege (beaten 10-0 on aggregate), Torino and Paris St Germain all succumbed and the stage was set for a classic final encounter with Parma, in Copenhagen.

The Danish city became a northern North Bank for the night, with Arsenal fans outnumbering their Italian counterparts by at least four to one. Although the odds were 3-1 against the London side winning, there was a definite feeling of defiance about this red and white army and nowhere was this more apparent than in Tony Adams. Bob Wilson, then BBC commentator, remembers him walking into breakfast on the morning of the match, looking like John Wayne. "You could see him thinking: 'This is the day of the battle'. Certainly, Arsenal were stretched by the skilful Italians and with Ian Wright suspended, goals were always likely to be scarce. However, Alan Smith, whose sense of occasion was still remarkably refined, scored a 19th- minute volley, and Arsenal hung on. It was to prove a last hurrah of sorts.

Another disappointing run in the league - though Arsenal still finished fourth - was perhaps more than made up for by that superb night in Copenhagen but the following season's performance, when they flirted with relegation before eventually finishing twelfth, confirmed that this was a team that had peaked. As Chris Lightblown in The Sunday Times wrote: "Arsenal have not only become a tactical dinosaur but a dinosaur built around the attributes of one player (Wright). The sort of side that slowly slips down league tables."

By February the writing was on the wall for Graham and his alleged financial indiscretions finally brought him down. His last game before being sacked was the 1-1 draw with Leicester City at Highbury. It was the type of supine result typical of those times but still an innocuous end to so mercurial an era. And although a second successive European Cup Winners' Cup Final was reached (and lost), under temporary manager Stewart Houston, the season will always be remembered for the day George Graham straightened his tie and walked out of Highbury for the very last time as Arsenal manager.

The stage now set for the emergence of today's great Arsenal side.

Arsenal Managers 1986-2000:

George Graham, 1986-1995

Bruce Rioch, 1995-1996

Arsene Wenger, 1996-

Picture Gallery

Michael Thomas scores the goal that won the 1988/89 championship for Arsenal in injury time at Anfield.

Kenny Sansom lifts the Littlewoods Cup for Arsenal after the 1987 final against Liverpool.

Alan Smith - goals on the big occasions.

At full stretch, Geoff Barnett can't stop Allan Clarke's header in the 1972 FA Cup Final.

Joe Baker, signed from Torino by Billy Wright to score goals for Arsenal.

David Seaman celebrates after the European Cup-Winners' Cup semi-final victory over Sampdoria, in which Sampdoria only scored twice in the penalty shoot-out.

A couple of suckers - John Radford and Peter Storey.

Fans celebrate the first trophy for 17 years at Highbury, to Frank McLintock's delight.

'My hero!' Charlie George.

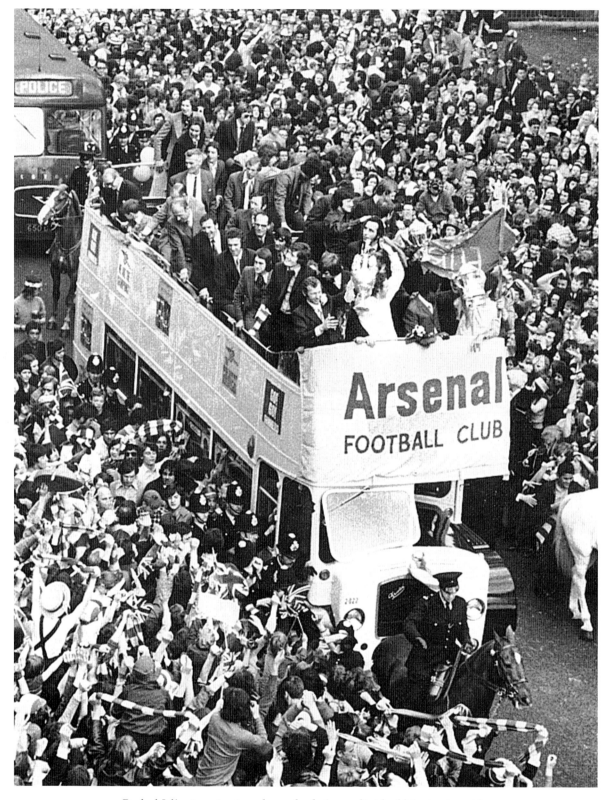

Packed Islington streets welcome back Arsenal's 'double' winning side.

Alan Sunderland

Herbert Chapman

Paul Merson and Gary Mabbutt, of Tottenham, challenge for the ball at Wembley.

Liam Brady